Caylie

LOOKING
FOR
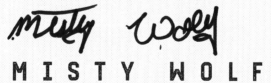

AN UNABASHED MEMOIR
OF THE BATTLE, BREAKTHROUGH,
AND FUTURE WITH A GENETIC VARIANT

Misty Wolf

MISTY WOLF

ISBN: 979-8-9850577-1-3 (Paperback)
ISBN: 979-8-9850577-2-0 (Hardcover)
ISBN: 979-8-9850577-0-6 (E-Book)

Library of Congress Control Number: 2021921333

Front cover image by Auri Cavendish
Book design by Vanessa Mendozzi

Printed by Misty Wolf, in the United States of America.

www.mistymwolf.com

Caylie,

you are my miracle

ACKNOWLEDGMENTS

Dr. Carl Fleisher—No matter how hard I was on you, how many times I said you weren't doing your job, or how many times I called your degrees worthless pieces of paper, you have always been there for Caylie and me. Your persistence and thoughtful process helped get Caylie back to living her life.

Lydia Mendoza Bauer—Thank you for saying "Yes" to Caylie when you were asked. Thank you for being there when I feared everything with Caylie's school. Thank you for picking up the phone all those nights when I was filled with worry. Even in the darkest days, you always saw the light in Caylie. Your love, passion, and dedication helped make Caylie the young woman she is today. Beyond that, it is an honor and privilege to call you my friend.

Nicole Niestrom—I was extremely hesitant about moving Caylie from Lydia's class as she finally achieved success. As it turns out, you and Lydia were right, and my fears were unwarranted. Caylie has only benefited from your kindness, creativity, and engaging life-skills courses. You always say you chose your career because your students are extraordinary in a world of ordinary. It is an honor and privilege to call you my friend today.

Geomara Salazar—You found unique ways to connect with Caylie, even when she wanted to be doing something else.

Emma Heatherington—When I signed up for a writing class, I never imagined having a teacher as unique as you. Thank you for your guidance and support throughout this entire book-writing process.

Victor Carone, Karlyn Johnson, Cristina Lavalle-Barry, and Marie Pierre—You never gave up on Caylie. You never gave up on me.

Shaun Butcher—My world is a better place because of you.

Cristina Florescu & Cassie Preston—Thank you for taking the time out of your hectic lives to provide insightful feedback, and helping me to take this story to the next level.

Glen & Kima Fair Cain, Emily R. Heger, Daniel "Dee" Harris, Jeff J Hunter, Molly Jones, Angel Jordan, Colette Letendre, Cheryl McGregor, the Nathan the Cat Lady, AP ladies, Satine Phoenix, Casandra & Melanie Rightmyer, Jamie "Chole" Robertson, and The Players Conservatory by Sean Maguire

CONTENTS

WE'VE CALLED THE
SHERIFF'S DEPARTMENT

When you become a mom, there is forever a piece of your heart out in the world. Try as you might, you will not be able to protect your child from everything. I expected stubbed toes, scraped knees, and maybe even a broken bone or two, but nothing prepared me for the phone call I received that Wednesday afternoon.

"What do you mean, 'Caylie is missing'?" I asked my mom. "I dropped her off at exactly eight-thirty this morning. I saw her walk through the door."

"Yes, they said Caylie was in her classes today."

"Okay, then what's the issue?"

"I think you should head over here, Misty."

If things had been usual, I'd have picked Caylie up after school today anyway. But my coursework was heavier for this six-week term, and I was determined to get through this degree on schedule. When Mom and Dad agreed to pick her up, it gave me the whole unbroken afternoon to work on assignments. Going to Caylie's school now, for example, would mean more research hours tonight when I seriously needed to sleep.

Suddenly what Mom had said sank in. Lack of sleep I could live with—but my daughter was missing? As the full realization hit me, my heart raced, and a chill up my spine reflected the late winter afternoon. Once the motor was running and I'd backed out, I pulled out my phone. Of course. Why hadn't either Mom or I thought of it? No doubt Caylie's father had picked her up and hadn't called to let me know.

Caylie would sometimes visit her father on Fridays, but today was Wednesday. Regardless, it wasn't fair to make assumptions. Instead, I decided to call him.

After three rings, there was the standard faint click to his voicemail.

"Please, please, please tell me you have Caylie," I recall trying to ask, but it came out begging, "Tell me you picked her up at school, and this is all a big miscommunication."

Silence.

Why silence?

It took longer than I cared to admit at that moment that, in reality, a voicemail is simply a recording service. I decided that a second phone call was necessary. Our child was missing, and I had questions only he could answer.

The second time through the voicemail, I knew I had to be clear and concise, "Please tell me if you picked up Caylie? If I misunderstood something or forgot something you said, say so."

We both vowed that, whatever else we did, we'd always stay in touch about Caylie. Maybe we'd talked about something special that would happen today. I didn't think so, but . . .

A text lit up, and I pulled over to read it.

"I have laryngitis," Caylie's father wrote. "I have no voice. If I did, I would be screaming. Where is Caylie?"

If I'd known where Caylie was, I would not be frantically phoning him, would I? I would not be begging to know she was with him. If I knew where she was, I would not be turning into the school parking lot at this moment, and I would know Mom and Dad had picked her up. If I knew where Caylie was, this whole day would not be turning into my personal horror story.

"When I know more, I'll text you," I answered, trying hard to sound more sympathetic than I felt.

Nothing seemed real. The ten-minute drive to Caylie's school felt like hours, like floating through a slow-motion movie, the tension rising second by second, every sound exaggerated—the crunch of a leaf underfoot, the faint swish of your running shoe on the asphalt. Just when you think you can't stand the wait any longer, you're in the building, and my Mom is there.

"What happened?" I asked.

"Your dad and I were over at Jack-In-The-Box getting dinner. We'd brought something for Caylie, and we were about three minutes late getting here. She wasn't where she always waits for us . . ."

"But Jack-In-The-Box is in the school parking lot. It shouldn't have made any difference . . ."

"It shouldn't have."

"So?"

Mom looked like she was about to cry. "They have people looking everywhere," she said, "and they're calling Caylie's teachers."

"Well, I dropped her off at school. I watched her go through that door—right there—and she walked past that desk—right there . . ."

"I know you did," Mom said, putting her hand on my arm. "Where's Dad?"

"He's going toward the 5 freeway and the Old Road."

"Why?"

"Maybe she went that way."

"Why would she go that way? I never go that way. She wouldn't know what was over there. Why would . . ."

"Your dad is just trying to find her, Misty. We're all just trying to find her."

Sometimes it takes longer for my brain to compute and process information in a way that makes logical sense. However, it was becoming abundantly clear that my thirteen-year-old, blond-haired, blue-eyed daughter was now a missing person. No one who would have been with Caylie or seen her on a typical school day had any idea where she could be.

While Mom looked downstairs, I ran up the stairs to where most of Caylie's classes were. I went through each of her classrooms and called her name, opening every door and closet. Desperation was setting in as I searched, and Caylie didn't appear with some sarcastic comment about being "right there."

There is a large multi-pane window that spans the upper and lower hallways of the school. When I'd searched every possible place Caylie could be, I looked out and realized that the afternoon light would only last a few more hours. While it had been moderately warm, the air would become cooler later in the afternoon. I knew what Caylie was wearing, that she would be cold if the wind kicked up. And did she have a water bottle? Panic was setting in.

I took the elevator down, and when I exited, the voice of Caylie's upper school principal broke through my foggy thoughts. I remember just staring at her, trying hard not to scream. I'm grateful I didn't say the words I was thinking.

The many voices around me were trying to give me information, effectively making it impossible to process what I was being told or asked. The voices turned to white noise as my panicking mind went through everything I knew to be a fact. Finally, I heard myself demand, "Where is my daughter?"

"We've called the sheriff's department, and we have everyone looking for her."

I could hear my heart beat loudly. It was impossible not to think of the countless television news stories that opened with the sheriff's department looking for a child. I bit my cheek hard enough to hurt before I thought of what to say.

"How could you possibly have lost my daughter?"

"Ms. Wolf, we know Caylie was in all of her classes, and we've called all of her teachers. Every one of them saw her walk out with the others in her class."

"Of course, she was in her classes. I watched her come in through the front door. It was your job to keep her safe until we picked her back up."

The principal looked beyond distressed. "Can we get you anything?" she asked. "A bottle of water, perhaps?"

"Changing the subject doesn't help," it was taking everything in my power to have a calm approach, "I moved Caylie here to give her the best education possible, and now she is missing."

"We're doing everything we can, Ms. Wolf. Everyone is working to find her."

There was nothing more for anyone to say to me. Mom had remained quiet throughout all this, and I silently thanked her for not trying to interfere.

A steady stream of people was coming in and out of the office. I didn't know who they were or why they were here. Soon, though, I recognized that two uniformed officers who'd just come in were sheriff's deputies—a man and a woman. The principal spoke to them and then brought them towards where Mom and I were sitting. I didn't feel like talking anymore, but I braced myself to cooperate. I knew that the two officers required information to help them with the search, and they would have to ask questions.

"Did Caylie seem upset today?" the uniformed young woman asked.

"She seemed fine. She loves to go to school."

"Does Caylie have a cellphone?"

"She had one, but she misused it with apps. I plan to get her another one, but I wanted to wait . . ."

"Her grandfather and I are getting it for her for Christmas," Mom interjected. It was news to me.

The guy was writing on a small, lined pad. "Did Caylie do drugs?" he asked, "or would she be looking for drugs?"

"No and no, she's a terrific kid who would rather be reading a book. . ."

"Never gets into trouble," Mom added.

"Is there any reason Caylie would want to run away?" the young woman asked.

I shook my head. "Caylie never spoke to me about running away for any reason. She has everything she could want, and she loves the bookstore and the library. She even collected books from the neighbors and made a library for her classmates at school."

"Are there friends she might have gone with?"

I was starting to reach my absolute limit with people asking me questions. I had developed a raging headache, and my politeness was continuing to dwindle, "No. Caylie is new to the school. She wouldn't just walk off with somebody she doesn't know."

"Just a couple more questions, Ms. Wolf," the young female officer continued. "We know you're tired. Has Caylie ever done this before?"

I wasn't tired, just incredulous that this was happening. Caylie wouldn't disappear on her own. Precious minutes were ticking away, and still, no one had found her.

"No, never," I said.

"The search and rescue team is on the way. They'll cover the area and the open spaces."

"Okay," I forced myself to say.

"And we need to get out an alert. Do you recall what Caylie was wearing?"

"She had on a flannel jacket when we left home this morning. You know, fuzzy with a hoodie. It was red plaid, like a kilt the Scottish wear. Her hair was in a lower ponytail, but sometimes she takes the hairband out. I think she wore her black pants today, too."

Usually, I wouldn't have remembered all the details, but Caylie and I had talked about getting her a different color jacket on the drive to school. She wanted a purple and black coat because it would go with one of her dresses. Caylie always liked fashion and having many different options in her closet. I found her fashion sense endearing.

Finally, the deputies went into the principal's office, where everyone else in the world seemed to have ended up.

I pulled out my cellphone. Unsurprisingly, there were tons of missed messages, most of them from Caylie's father. I tried to write him a response and deleted it no fewer than a dozen times. What could I say? Nothing made sense enough to hit the send button. Whatever I wrote would end up being another, *I don't know.*

The office door kept opening and closing, with people coming in and out. Each time the door opened, I could see a growing crowd of people inside. If everyone was looking for Caylie, why was the office full of people?

The slow-motion of the past two-and-a-half hours continued, with the kind of frozen silence you feel when people walk by you and won't make eye contact. I scrolled through local news pages on my phone. Caylie's missing-person story was not there yet. Was that a positive or a negative sign? Was it just not unusual enough, not important enough to make the evening headlines?

Mom had walked over to the principal's office. She was acting more as a liaison, giving me updates. She was the best person they could have in that role. I would have been too frustrated with anyone else to bite my tongue.

"Is Dad back?" I asked her.

"You know your dad. He won't come back as long as Caylie is out there somewhere."

"I know."

"And if she doesn't come back."

"Mom, Caylie's coming back!"

For the first time today, I saw tears in her eyes, "Please don't cry. Because if you start crying, I'm going to shatter into a million pieces."

Her strength and level-headed approach kept me from panicking. Mom also kept me from leaving the office to look for Caylie myself or calling the press to get Caylie's picture and information into the community. Across the hall, people continued to hover, and Mom made her way back to listen.

When I was left alone, endless questions with no answers kept banging through my head. What had I missed with Caylie to bring us to this point? Caylie had always come to me with any questions or concerns, or a list of things she wanted to go out shopping to get.

I saw Mom come out of the principal's office into the adjoining office, and suddenly people were pouring out behind her. Mom was smiling all over, and I heard the words, "They found her!"

I was afraid to ask the hovering question but finally blurted it out. "Is Caylie alive?"

"Yes!" Mom's voice was heavy with relief. "They're bringing

her back to the school."

"Where did they find her?"

"I'm not sure. I know that whoever found Caylie called the principal, and they are on their way back to the school."

Then the door closed again. Until that day, I'd never known how much you could resent a door being closed. I wanted to yell, "Stop closing the door! It's my daughter you're talking about!" But I was too tired, too emotional . . . and too afraid of what might be ahead.

It turned out that I, her mom, would not be the first to see Caylie. Instead, the two sheriff's deputies would be. Of course, that made sense. Maybe she would tell them where she had been, and why. Perhaps then I would have something to tell Caylie's father, to make sense of the past three hours.

The annoying headache that had plagued me had turned into a full-blown migraine by this point. All I wanted to do was hug my daughter and go home. Instead, I realized that I was watching the clock on the wall.

Half an hour later, the deputies opened the door and brought Caylie into the room where Mom and I had been waiting. When I saw her and saw that she was okay, I couldn't hold back the tears. There she stood with her red plaid jacket and her backpack, looking at me as if nothing had happened. All I could say was, "Why?"

"Because you were late!"

"Three minutes. Three whole minutes, Caylie."

"I wanted to go home, and it was time to go home."

"Grandma and Grandpa were getting you something to eat."

"They were late."

It had quickly become a pointless argument. I would need to find a better way to communicate with Caylie. That conversation could wait. It was necessary now to ensure that she felt loved, despite her wayward adventure. I stood up and hugged her, thanking every God or overarching deity that had kept her safe.

The sheriff's deputies finally gave me the complete story. Caylie told them that I was late, and she wanted to go home. She had walked to the crosswalk near the school, used the crosswalk light, and followed the road, "She knew the way, but there was some flaw in her logic about navigating the freeway."

"The freeway?"

A teacher, Malaka Donovan, found Caylie walking down the wrong side of the 126 freeway. The two deputies had concluded that she was just a determined teen who had been reckless, and nothing was amiss. We were free to go.

'Free to go' was relative in this situation. I finally drafted a text message to Caylie's father with all the details. Like me, Caylie's father found it unbelievable that Caylie would walk away from her school.

"Caylie, I don't care if it's me or Grandma and Grandpa who are late," I told her. "You do not walk on freeways! Period. End of sentence. Do you understand me?"

"Can we go home now?"

"Caylie, you could have been taken away by a stranger! Do you understand?"

"I want to go home, Mom."

It was clear that Caylie lacked any understanding or fear of the danger she'd put herself in by walking on a freeway.

I DON'T KNOW

n the weeks following Caylie's disappearance from school, things that had seemed so routine with Caylie had to be adapted and changed. Gone were the days when adults in all parts of her life could trust her judgment. Everything about her life now demands that she is with a responsible adult at all times and that she is handed off by each adult to another adult to ensure one-hundred-percent supervision and accountability.

This meant that there were three adults in our house who could supervise Caylie. I took the lion's share of the time, finding much of my sleeping time when she was at school. My parents took over when I was working on homework assignments or away for appointments. I was on duty at night, until four in the morning, when Mom took over until I took Caylie to school.

Taking Caylie to school each morning meant parking out front and walking with her to the first teacher on her schedule. Caylie was angry about this sudden invasion of adults constantly with her. She didn't understand why she was no longer allowed to collect shiny pebbles or unique-looking tree leaves before school or during recess. I understood her frustration, but until I could be sure of what had caused her out-of-character behavior, changes were necessary to keep her safe.

The Individualized Education Program (IEP) support team at Caylie's school was helpful in ensuring that Caylie was continuing her education. Caylie had been on an IEP since 2nd grade, due to ADHD. At her current school, Victor Carone, Caylie's educational support coordinator from February 2017 to August 2018, became the final voice I trusted regarding Caylie's school programs. Now that Caylie had Victor actively overseeing her education, I could find a psychiatrist to help with her mental health.

Around this time, Caylie began talking under her breath about things I didn't understand. It often felt like our conversations resembled a game in which Caylie had the rule book, and the rules changed without notice. Caylie was adamant that whatever she told me about was real to her, but it made no sense when she explained it. If I asked her about it, she would raise her voice in frustration, saying that I knew, and I was lying.

So many times throughout this sudden mysterious takeover of my daughter's mind, I wondered what she was thinking. Could she tell me if she was scared?

No.

Could we talk long enough to help me understand?

That was also a No.

Did Caylie know that I was always on her side, and only on her side, no matter what?

No answer.

Meanwhile, life doesn't stop for anyone to play catch up. Instead, everyone around Caylie—teachers and family—looked to me to provide insight. It made sense for everyone to assume that I should know what was going on with Caylie, but in reality, it was the furthest thing from the truth. You never know how small you can feel until you hear yourself answering, "I don't know," to question after question…

But how could I know?

I had so many questions myself, and no one to answer them. I was still trying to find a psychiatrist who would even take Caylie on as a patient. Everybody assumed that it would be easy, with so many psychiatrists in the Los Angeles area. Instead, the outlook seemed to fall somewhere between discouraging and impossible. Flipping through the thousands of psychiatrists who surface in an internet search is daunting.

Many people around me didn't realize that I was still dealing with negative feelings towards psychiatry in general. While it had been well over a decade, my mom's former psychiatrist, in my view, had failed her. Though this did teach me a valuable life lesson: it was critical to research how a doctor viewed treating the patient as a whole person, versus only whatever illness ailed them. Regardless of my underlying mistrust of psychiatry, Caylie needed help, and she depended on me to find it. I couldn't fail.

Fortunately, I knew precisely the skill-set that I wanted and expected for Caylie's future doctor. The psychiatrist for my Caylie would be highly recommended, and experienced in working with adolescents. He or she would be absolutely the top-rated professional available in their field. They would treat Caylie from a psychiatry perspective, but never lose sight of the fact that Caylie should be allowed to live her life to the fullest as a young teen.

As Caylie's advocate, I wanted her treatment plan and treatment goals to be clear, with a list of possible outcomes. I understood that a mental health diagnosis could be complex, but it was necessary to educate myself and prepare myself for the many possible scenarios that awaited us. Most of all, I did not want my daughter to be over-medicated, as it would effectively render her a prisoner in her own body. I wanted her to live a whole, happy life with as little medical intervention as possible.

I started researching psychiatrists who were alumni of Yale, Harvard, Stanford, Princeton, UCLA, USC, and Columbia University. I compiled the main list, and added more psychiatrists local to California who had strong qualifications, even if they weren't from the top medical universities. I would leave no stone unturned to ensure that I would find Caylie the best psychiatrist for her case.

The first few days of my search produced page after page of profiles of psychiatrists whose descriptions seemed to meet Caylie's requirements. Next, I sought reviews from patients on reputable medical sites to match each doctor's profile. Finally, I went through my entire information collection, and narrowed down the list, based on their clients' reviews and the methodology used to treat them.

Finally, I believed that Caylie was one step closer to having a psychiatrist who had the approach I wanted for her treatment. Having whittled my list down from my vast initial base of potential doctors for Caylie, it had become clear that Doctor Carl Fleisher was absolutely the top choice.

Dr. Fleisher, a graduate of Harvard, completed his residency in adult psychiatry. He taught psychiatry there, then joined the UCLA Department of Psychiatry and Biobehavioral Sciences as an assistant clinical professor. As well as teaching at UCLA in Los Angeles, Dr. Fleisher also practiced there.

In addition to his official qualifications, he described his treatment approach as evidence-based and holistic. A patient's treatment plan would consist of clear, measurable goals for improvement. The goals I had set were now realistic possibilities for Caylie. She would, indeed, have the most qualified psychiatrist for her case in Dr. Fleisher.

In addition, UCLA also offered one of the best hospitals anywhere for mental health—The Stewart and Lynda Resnick Neuropsychiatric Hospital. We had the best doctor for Caylie, and one of the best hospitals right within our driving distance—everything Caylie and I could have hoped for, and more.

I was actually in tears when I dialed the number to make an appointment for Caylie. Tears of happiness and relief, or tears of fear? Maybe a combination of all three. A few rings later, a kind voice greeted me on the call, and I summoned up my courage, because nothing had been easy in our journey.

"I need to make an appointment," I said.

"No problem. Can I get the patient's birthdate?"

"I meant, she's not yet a patient. My daughter is a new patient. Could we start over? I need to make an appointment for my daughter with Dr. Carl Fleisher."

"Of course you can. Tell me about your daughter."

"My daughter's name is Caylie Moore, and she's a new patient. I know that she has ADHD that's not under control, but something else is wrong. She recently walked away from school and went missing. She's talking to herself, which I thought maybe was okay, but I think now that I was wrong. Does Dr. Fleisher still take patients? I need Dr. Fleisher to see Caylie."

I'd said all that without coming up for air. At one point, I knew I sounded like I was crying. Nothing had gone right since I picked up the phone. I took a deep breath and listened to the kind voice at the other end.

"Yes, Dr. Fleisher is taking clients," the voice said. "The way the process works is, we make two appointments, one with the family, then two days later, an interview with the patient."

The friendly voice gave me two appointments, March 22nd, and March 24th. I had done it. I had found the help Caylie needed, and she was on the way to getting her life back.

Or so I thought.

HARD TO BELIEVE

E ven though Caylie had been returned safely to us on that terrifying day in February, I realized that I was still looking for her—the Caylie I had known and loved for fifteen years. Down underneath this façade she was wearing, the real Caylie was still there, and she would reappear the same way we had lost her—suddenly and without explanation. I never doubted that she would return.

As it does with all of us, Caylie's genetic inheritance may have dumped a load of baggage for her to carry. When you are a desperate parent looking for answers, you start to ask everyone in your family what mental illness they might have. In truth, it is one of the most uncomfortable questions to ask your family, and I felt so intrusive.

On Caylie's paternal side, her father's relatively quick response was that nothing ran in his family. I often wondered if that were true, but pushing the issue harder was not in Caylie's best interests, so I chose to accept it.

I knew that my genetics may have been a little more complex because I had always dealt with an obsessive-compulsive personality disorder. My Mom has a borderline personality disorder or bipolar disorder, and owing to similarities in symptoms, it is difficult to say which it is, for sure. There is also another unknown layer in the genetic equation for Caylie, as my Mom is an adoptee from Seoul, Korea, and at that time, we had no information on what else ran in her genes.

Meanwhile, I have one cousin who has Tourette syndrome and another with schizoaffective disorder on my paternal family's side. I lost count of the hours I spent diving into medical journals and studies to understand the complex world of mental health. The stark reality was that Caylie's life's recent direction had taken a turn that was different from anything my family members had experienced.

From the beginning, going to school had been an extra challenge for Caylie, but one she took on with courage, kindness, and spirit. As early as preschool and kindergarten, her teachers and other school staff recognized her need for an Individualized Education Plan (IEP). In truth, I wish I could say that I always understood and embraced the idea of Caylie's requiring extra help in school, but I didn't.

Caylie was my only child, and in my eyes, Caylie was beautiful and perfect when she went to school. When educators would suggest to me that she was different, or required extra help, I was puzzled. What could be wrong with a kind, sweet little girl who said please and thank you? Was it that abnormal? In truth, I think it was the memory of my school days and how schools handled students with disabilities that gave me a fear of Caylie's having one.

When Caylie was in second grade, her teacher, Mrs. Rhinda Cook, explained that Caylie seemed to understand the work, but couldn't sit still long enough to complete it. I think Mrs. Cook's approach made me less fearful and defensive than I had been. I finally was confident enough to take additional steps with Caylie's general pediatrician.

Caylie at that time was given the diagnosis of Attention Deficit Hyperactive Disorder (ADHD). I remember crying the day I had to start giving Caylie her medication. I didn't want Caylie to be dependent on medication to live her life to the fullest. That said, I would always do the right thing by Caylie, and my research indicated that people with ADHD had notable improvement on medication.

Mrs. Cook began to see improvements: Caylie now retained information she had learned, but hadn't previously been able to express. At this point, we started the IEP testing process to help Caylie continue to thrive throughout her time in school. By the end of second grade, I had become grateful for the extra educational resources Caylie received owing to her IEP.

Caylie had always tried to do well, and, with her IEP, she went from trying to do well to thriving, and enjoying her learning experience. The IEP team even thought she might return to general education in her pre- and early-teen years. It's hard for people who haven't known her very long to believe it, but she was so sweet, and so much fun. I miss that part of her. It makes me sad that most people never knew that side of Caylie.

For Caylie, though, her thirteenth year was to bring a stark life change.

IT'S LIKE THE MOVIES

The famous Getty Center sits high atop the often lush, rolling hills of the Sepulveda Pass, overlooking Interstate 405. What should be a beautiful, scenic drive through the Pass is instead bumper-to-bumper traffic, countless car accidents, and never-ending lane closures, often citing some maintenance work. The Interstate 405 freeway is without question one of the worst commutes in California.

As I sat barely rolling along with thousands of other people, I had the unpleasant realization that this would be part of every trip to the UCLA campus. How had I forgotten about the 405 parking lot with all my diligent planning and research? Of all the things, it would be a significant source of annoyance for the foreseeable future.

Countless times during this initial two-hour drive, I wanted to turn around and go home. On the one hand, I knew I should be excited that I was finally meeting someone who would help Caylie. On the other, I felt awful. I had a sinking feeling I would find a way to ruin the process. Should I just go back home, rather than possibly making anything worse?

As internal war raged between fighting for Caylie or fleeing, eventually, I decided that running was a cowardly reaction, and I didn't have time to be a coward. Caylie relied on me to be a strong advocate for her. She deserved the best chance to get her life back on track, which started now, at this appointment with Dr. Fleisher. If I didn't push through the fear and fight to find out why she was sick, would anyone else care enough to help her?

Parking around UCLA is a nightmare. The school and medical offices have a fee-based parking structure that costs at least $13, if not more. I wasn't aware of the parking fees at UCLA before I arrived. By sheer luck, my mom had given me $20 to refill my gas tank. While I'd recently started my small business in crystal sales, it took time to build up clients. Every dollar counted, and spending at least $13 to park, instead of filling the tank with gas, was not what I'd expected.

By the time I'd parked, I was in tears. Absolutely nothing was going right, and I couldn't imagine this critical appointment for Caylie's future would either. As I walked to the nearest sign by the staircase, I wiped away my tears only to discover that I needed another building entirely. I grew increasingly frustrated that I was still wholly lost, despite walking around the entire floor.

Fifteen minutes later, I walked through the sliding doors of Building 300. If it could go wrong today, it seemingly had gone wrong, and emotionally I couldn't be sure that anything would suddenly go right. As I stared at the double doors to the office, I wondered why I was even here. If I didn't fit in here with the fancy doctors of UCLA, then neither would Caylie. It would have been so easy to give in to my fears; I wouldn't have needed much to push me in that direction.

What Is a Psychiatrist?

The American Psychiatric Association describes *psychiatry* as the branch of medicine focused on diagnosing, treating, and preventing mental, emotional, and behavioral disorders. A *psychiatrist* is a medical doctor (M.D. or D.O.) who specializes in these areas of mental health. As a physician, a psychiatrist can prescribe medications and apply other approaches to patient treatment.

When might a person or their family member seek treatment by a psychiatrist?

A person might look for a psychiatrist when they have experienced a panic attack, hallucinations, hearing voices, persistent anxiety, or difficulty controlling their behavior with others.

Diagnosing patients: A psychiatrist may order a wide range of medical laboratory and psychological tests. Along with interviews with the patient, family members, and professionals who interact with the patient, the test results help the psychiatrist assess the patient's mental health and behavioral problems. Specific diagnoses are described in APA's *Diagnostic and Statistical Manual of Mental Disorders (DSM-5)*.

Psychiatric therapy: Among the types of treatment used by psychiatrists are "talk therapy" and medication. Research labs have developed and tested medications that affect a patient's mental and psychological functioning in specific ways. The psychiatrist may prescribe medications that can

improve the patient's ability to manage their feelings
and behavior. In talk therapy, the psychiatrist engages
the patient in conversations designed to increase the
patient's awareness of the patterns of thinking that
may be causing or exacerbating their functional and
social difficulties.

The check-in desk was one of the larger ones I'd encountered, as it weaved slightly, much like a small wave. There were two workstations, and a small office printer set up behind them. The friendly receptionist gave me the standard intake packet, and I paid the usual co-payment for Caylie's insurance.

Once I returned the intake packet to the receptionist, it was back to sitting in silence. If you've ever sat in a waiting room, you know how tedious the waiting time can be. However, the fear and apprehension you're feeling can be even worse. I read every magazine within reach, and scrolled through my cell phone, but I still couldn't shake the anxiety.

Finally, after a long wait, a moderate baritone voice called Caylie's name. Dr. Carl Fleisher was behind that baritone voice, and I met him by the hallway door. We shook hands and exchanged pleasantries. He was about six feet tall, with bright blue eyes and a warming smile. As we walked down the hall towards his office, I could feel the anxiety fading. Finally, I was starting to build a team to help Caylie get back to living her life.

"Tell me about your daughter," he said once we had settled into his office.

"My daughter has this typically beautiful, loving, and kind personality. Anyone who has ever met her would tell you she was helpful, and always reached out to people. Caylie has the most infectious personality, and you can't help but laugh or smile with her."

"Is there anything you remember that could have caused her behavior to go downhill?"

"Mr. Bennett, her music teacher, was killed by a hit-and-run driver just before the summer break (May 2016). Grandpa, sorry, my Grandpa, who was her Great Grandpa, passed away earlier in the year (February 2016). Caylie seemed to understand that with a funeral, you were saying goodbye. I didn't see anything that concerned me in her reactions."

"Can you describe the behaviors you've been seeing?"

It was the last thing I wanted to do. I had been trying to forget the strange behaviors coming from my daughter. When Caylie could no longer verbally say what she required, it left bruises, nail claw scratches, and sometimes bite marks as her method of communication. But if he was to help Caylie, Dr. Fleisher needed to know.

"She has violent or aggressive moments when she kicks, scratches, and bites while she's yelling in a language that doesn't make sense."

"Can you clarify what it is about the language that doesn't make sense?"

" I thought she might be possessed—you know, like in the movies? I even asked my mom's priest about it. He said she was not possessed. But when she talks, it's about things on the 'other side'? The hard part is I have no idea what the other side is or what she means when she says it. She also sometimes uses a high-pitched sound, almost like a flute that's poorly tuned."

"Is she pretending to be playing the flute when she makes that sound?"

"It's just her voice. She gets louder and higher-pitched, and the more upset she gets, the louder she gets. Honestly, it hurts my ears, depending on how long she goes on with the noise."

"Do other members of the family say anything to you about

Caylie's behavior?"

"They're very upset about it. My parents, uncles, and aunts often ask *why is Caylie acting so strange? What are you going to do about Caylie's behavior?* They aren't very supportive of my going to a psychiatrist because they believe psychiatry is a theoretical science, which isn't entirely wrong, based on their experiences. But I'm here, going against everyone else because I think you are the person who can best help my daughter."

"Thank you, and I will certainly strive to help Caylie become healthy again."

STOP TALKING ABOUT ME!

Caylie's intake visit with Dr. Fleisher took place on March 24th. Interstate 405 proved once again that it would always be a miserable drive. When I looked in the rear-view mirror, Caylie made faces and whispered under her breath, and attempting to have a conversation with her only ended up with angry mumbles.

While I'd driven through this same parking structure two days ago, I had not memorized the layout. Meanwhile, Caylie was growing restless in the back seat. If nothing else, Caylie and I agreed that we couldn't be late. It took another ten minutes to find a car leaving, but at least we could finally park.

I always thought that Caylie would have made an excellent sprinter, as she was always twenty steps ahead of me.

"Caylie, you're too far ahead; slow down."

"I'm right here. You can see me with your eyes."

"Yes, but you are half a mile ahead of me."

The check-in process went quickly, and Caylie found amusement in the children's area. Thankfully, I heard Dr. Fleisher call Caylie's name about ten minutes later, and she went to talk to him without much of an argument. Caylie and Dr. Fleisher would have a one-on-one session that lasted about thirty minutes, followed by a group meeting with me.

It wasn't long before Dr. Fleisher called me into the second part of the meeting, and we would determine the next steps for Caylie's treatment. Dr. Fleisher went over his findings, and as a team, we decided to work on helping Caylie with her ADHD. As previous doctors had been able to help Caylie to live successfully with ADHD, logically, it should continue to be treatable with a medication adjustment.

Caylie began her regular appointments with Dr. Fleisher in April 2017. Over the coming months, Dr. Fleisher would experience Caylie's ups and downs, and her vast array of concerning behaviors. I knew that Caylie was making a sincere effort to find her way, in a mental matrix that she couldn't cope with alone.

In retrospect, it was only when I started writing Caylie's story that I read for the first time what Dr. Fleisher had written in his notes from Caylie's and my initial visit. He had put in a great effort, he wrote, to answer questions and manage the emotions of a sick child. Even in 2021, it reaffirmed what I already knew about Dr. Fleisher: he was the best doctor for Caylie.

As Caylie's appointments continued regularly, each one became an all-day ordeal. Caylie hated anyone interrupting her day, or any of her routines. Today's appointment was no exception. Unlike the last few appointments, which had just been Caylie and me, my mother wanted to talk to Caylie's doctor.

I welcomed anyone who could give Dr. Fleisher more information, and I gladly took Mom with us. As if the process weren't already an ordeal to manage, Mom obviously had an agenda for joining us, making it even more challenging. In the early days of Caylie's appointments, the two-hour drive had been primarily peaceful. Caylie enjoyed listening to pop music, or sometimes musicals, in the car, and I made new mixed CDs to keep her entertained. My Mom, on the other hand, seemed annoyed by the car ride.

Of course, everyone was worried about Caylie, and each of us showed our stress differently. She showed hers via her role as a passenger.

"What's wrong?" I asked her.

"I want to make sure this doctor understands what is going on with Caylie."

"Don't be rude to him; he's the best there is. Trust me, I looked through so many profiles of great doctors, but he's the best."

"I'm not going to be rude."

"I know you, Mom."

"But we haven't seen any improvements."

"Mom, it's been one whole month. It's not magic."

"Well, I'm going to tell him what I think."

"He's a good doctor, and he wants to help. I like the process. I want to ensure that my kid, whatever's wrong…."

"*STOP TALKING ABOUT ME!!!*" came from the back seat.

"Oh, I'm sorry, Caylie. We were just…."

"*Talking about me!*"

"Do you want me to change it to the next song, Cay?"

"Number 8."

I changed the CD to music track number 8, and Caylie seemed happy for the moment. It was always hard to know when Caylie was listening to our conversations. Sometimes she was engaged, and at others, she was having conversations with herself. Then there were the times I wanted to talk to her about what she was experiencing, but nothing she said made sense.

Each time we came to UCLA, the pay-for-parking model would upset me. I asked one of the medical receptionists during check-in, and even they were required to pay the price to park. It seems unreasonable to add the cost of parking to patients, let alone to employees, when UCLA is widely known to be profitable. After finding parking, which was never easy in the private fee-based parking structure, we walked to the 300 building.

"Caylie, slow down."

"I'm right here!"

"I see that, but you are walking too fast."

"Well, that's bullshit! You're lying!"

"We don't say those words."

"Yes, yes we do. Yes, we say them! When things are like that, on the other side."

"There is no other side, Caylie. There's just here and now."

I knew that statement would cause a disagreement.

"That's bullshit. That's bullshit."

"That's enough now, Caylie."

"No, it's not enough!"

It was time to try to redirect the escalating behavior.

"Time to go check-in."

I pulled open the door to the office. I was grateful that when we went into the main office, Caylie never caused a scene. The office had standard magazines and a table with coloring books and crayons. Caylie enjoyed reading the books and coloring, and they would pass the time as we waited.

After getting Caylie checked in, I took a seat beside Mom to watch Caylie. Oddly, these were silent moments, the ones I had come to hate the most. The guilt, fear, anger, and anxiety all bubbled up in the silence, and made me feel very small. But I know it doesn't matter how I think: my daughter feels worse.

Playing in the doctor's office seemed to give Caylie peace. It was rare for her not to talk to herself now, but, at least here, other patients spoke aloud to themselves, too. It might not be the outside world's version of normal, but here, Caylie and I weren't alone with an invisible illness.

Dr. Fleisher's voice called for Caylie, and she responded, pushing by him to head towards his office. I followed behind her, talking with Dr. Fleisher on the way. Once we were in the office, Caylie and Mom took the long couch, and I took the chair next to the bookcase. Dr. Fleisher's desk was across from all of us, with a small cabinet on the right side.

Dr. Fleisher started the meeting off pleasantly. "How are things going with Caylie?"

"I don't see any changes," I said. "Caylie continues to be unreasonable and aggressive, and refuses to listen to even basic things. Caylie was never like this; she was kind-hearted and sweet. I know it doesn't seem like it, but I'm telling you, something isn't right."

"Misty has overly high expectations of Caylie," my Mom chimed in.

I remember looking at my Mom as if she were an alien that had grown a third head. What was she saying? In what world did I have unreasonable expectations? My kid had walked away from school on a freeway. She had also hit, scratched, and bitten me. I believed something was wrong, and I expected someone to help me to find the answer.

"Caylie lost her Great-Grandpa last year," Mom continued, "and her Grammy about five years before that. Her band teacher was also killed in a hit and run last year. It's a lot for a child to deal with."

If ever I wanted to disappear, now would have been that moment. I now knew how this conversation was about to go. I put my head in my hands, just listening and trying to be respectful.

"So, do you think it's normal that someone walks on a freeway?" Dr. Fleisher's calm voice inquired of Mom.

I remember counting the squares on the carpet. I could not in my wildest dreams have predicted Caylie's appointment going this way. I already blamed myself for Caylie's being sick, and now, it appeared, my Mom blamed me too. I wondered if Dad, also, believed it was my fault.

How many people thought my daughter's illness was my fault in my small world?

"I have raised three kids," Mom continued, "and I think this is normal early teenage behavior, exploring boundaries and testing how far they can go."

I'd had enough. "Look, all I know is that my daughter was one way, and now she is another. Yes, it's true, I haven't raised other kids, but I grew up with many cousins. I've seen what people consider normal behavioral patterns, and this isn't normal. But actually, I don't even require that she be whatever the normal standard is! I just want her to be the best person she can be."

I wouldn't know until years later what Dr. Fleisher was writing in his notes at this time, but I hoped something positive would come from my Mom's assertions. I didn't even care if he said Mom was right, and that I had no idea. I was completely fine with being wrong. My only hope was that Dr. Fleisher would find something in what Mom had said to give him insight into helping Caylie.

Hope was a fragile thing, but it was all I had. The more pieces of the puzzle we collected for Caylie, the better things would become. The power of being positive was a thread I could hold on to, and no one could take it away.

"Were you able to get the SNAP paperwork from the teachers?" Dr. Fleisher inquired.

"No, I emailed them in, but I need to follow up on it. I have it on my to-do list. Can I email it directly to you after I get replies? Or do they have to be a hard copy?"

The SNAP paperwork was simply a standardized question-set to diagnose attention deficit hyperactivity disorder. It would help Dr. Fleisher get the teacher's perspective on improving our treatment plan for Caylie. I felt like a project manager all over again. My daughter's illness had become a project for which I had paperwork and deadlines. At least having to collect paperwork on a deadline was something that made sense to me.

Dr. Fleisher advised that I could email the paperwork once I received it.

We said our goodbyes, and made an appointment for a return visit in four weeks. As we walked back to the car, I looked at Mom and shook my head,

"I literally cannot believe you said that."

"I said what I felt was true."

"But did you have to make me think that I am the only one seeing this? Come on; she left school!"

"Sometimes you left school, too."

"There is a big difference between calling you to come home and walking on a freeway."

"*STOP TALKING ABOUT ME!*"

There was a young person in the back seat who had feelings. It was easy to forget that sometimes Caylie would follow our conversations. Of all the discussions about her, I wished that she could have remained blissfully unaware of this one.

"We were more or less talking about me, but that's okay. Are you hungry?"

"I want orange chicken but not the orange chicken from the sushi place, real orange chicken from Panda Express."

"Panda Express it is, kiddo."

THE BOOKSTORE

I f anyone deserved retirement, Dad did. Dad went straight from high school into the military, and then into his lifelong career with the phone company. While working full-time at the phone company, Dad still found time to manage my brother's baseball teams and attend Woodbury University.

In May 2007, at 54 years old, my dad graduated from Woodbury as the class valedictorian. Watching his perseverance as he obtained A+ after A+ was nothing short of inspirational. If I am honest, I went to Ashford University because my dad proved that you were never too old to get an education.

It seemed like a great idea when Dad decided to remodel the house to suit his retirement life. The house had survived three kids, with countless dogs, and it had earned a facelift. At first, the remodel would be a breeze, but the reality of the task was exhausting to everyone. Starting in late March 2017, the work was still going on in the sweltering heat of August.

"Mom," Caylie's voice broke into my rare morning peace. "They're in the backyard again." She came into my room bringing her tablet, and stood there staring at me as if she expected me to move them somewhere else.

"I know, Baby. They'll be done soon, I'm sure."

"That's a *lie*. You're *lying*. They're never leaving!"

Days when Caylie was happy were becoming few and far between. The last thing I needed was another day of Caylie's being upset. I was already feeling worthless because I'd caused us to miss our appointment with Dr. Fleisher in May. I'd written it in the wrong place on the calendar. How could I fail at my one job in life?

Hard as it was, I'd stopped caring whether other people thought I was lazy and disorganized. I put all my energy into my daughter and helping her become healthy again. Fortunately, they let me rebook in early August.

Caylie had loved to spend time in the yard, and I understood that the renovation work had taken this away from her. The remodel to the backyard would add a walkway, with planters full of roses. Beyond that, there would be brand new green grass for Caylie to dance around on. When it came to the design, Dad put a great deal of thought into it.

"Caylie, they'll be done soon," I said, wanting to be encouraging, "and you'll like the backyard even better, I promise."

"That's a lie. Stop telling lies!" She reached out and swatted my arm.

"We don't hit people," I reminded her. "That's not nice to do."

"But it's on the other side!"

By now, I had learned that talking about the other side would almost always escalate into a significant argument. It was better to change the subject and de-escalate the atmosphere. As Caylie loved the local bookstores, suggesting a bookstore adventure had a good chance of upstaging the backyard disaster.

"How about this," I ventured. "If you go get ready, we can go to the bookstore. Would you like that?"

"The Open Book, or Barnes & Noble?" Caylie's bright blue eyes seemed to be considering her subsequent response.

"I hadn't figured that part out yet. Where would you like to go?"

"The Open Book!"

"Then the Open Book it is."

The Open Book is a unique used-book store in our town. Its wall-to-wall books cover every imaginable type and topic. The store's layout allows you to wander and discover things you might never have thought of reading. The Open Book gave Caylie a public place to be herself and consider what she wanted to purchase.

The staff at The Open Book are a great group of young adults who foster reading in all young people. They had come to know Caylie. She sought out the display of new books and searched through them intently. Before long, The Open Book started a painting night, and Caylie would always remind me to go. The Open Book was her favorite place, and I believed it was because the staff made her feel welcomed.

While Caylie shopped, I enjoyed the journal section near the front door. Caylie could always find me there when she was ready to check out. The rare days where Caylie was happy during this time relieved me, because I could become a parent advocate.

If I could revisit the challenging year 2017 had become, I would make myself a standard call log to establish a detailed record of every call and response from agencies or people. Having a simple call log would have allowed me to coordinate a follow-up system and, if necessary, have a reference point for case escalation. However, it would be two years before I discovered how to create a formal bookkeeping system for Caylie.

Meanwhile, our last visit with Dr. Fleisher had been in March. He was eager for Caylie to go through the Child and Adult Neurodevelopmental Clinic (CAN) for formal testing.

UCLA is a gigantic research and medical complex in a bulging megalopolis. It's hard to know if anyone gets the messages you leave in any office that you call. After calling at least twice, and getting no response, I felt discouraged. Becoming an advocate for Caylie taught me the hard way to toughen up for the long road ahead.

As the summer of 2017 marched forward, Caylie and I arrived at the August appointment with Dr. Fleisher. As I sat across from him, I couldn't believe what he said.

"I thought Autism Spectrum Disorder became obvious when children were small," I protested, "maybe one or two years old."

"The ADHD diagnosis was understandable. She was a healthy child except for her inability to remain focused, but a lot was going on beyond ADHD."

"So what you're saying is that if our family physician had referred her to a psychiatrist, they might have gotten it right."

"It is difficult to know if it would have made a difference in Caylie's current situation."

Since Caylie had become ill, my mental health research into finding cases similar to Caylie's had been exhaustive. I wanted Dr. Fleisher to know that I wasn't ignorant of the state of mental diagnoses when Caylie was six years old.

"We both know," I said, "that no doctor, psychiatrist or not, could have made a dual diagnosis at the time that Caylie was declared ADHD. The rules of psychiatry didn't allow it in 2009."

"It's true. The American Psychiatric Association's diagnostic manual in 2013 was the update that allowed doctors to use multiple diagnoses."

"Right, and at the time of her ADHD diagnosis, Caylie showed no sign of anything else at home or at school," I said. "Caylie was making progress on what she was behind in, and overall was thriving socially. She was an amazing person. She has always been an amazing person, even if you aren't able to see it right now."

"I know it's upsetting. It's a process of understanding what we are dealing with now. It's going to take time."

"Autism is so easy to blame when you can't explain the symptoms. Just because Caylie is neurodivergent does not automatically mean that she is autistic."

"It's one of many things Caylie presents. Testing will help me understand more, and work towards an effective treatment plan for Caylie."

"I'm telling you that Caylie doesn't just magically have autism. I'll accept autism, but only while you keep gathering evidence and test results. I refuse to believe it's just autism, and I'm not giving up until you give me something that makes sense."

I would be lying if I said I wasn't mad. I'd lived through the 1990s when doctors seemed to think everyone had ADHD. Once science had realized that the diagnosis had become overused, it became difficult to get treatment for that diagnosis. It seemed to me that autism had now become the new ADHD.

As I listened to Dr. Fleisher explain the details of Autism Spectrum Disorder, I was trying not to cry, simply from anger and frustration. I knew what autism was, and I knew that, while we could manage the symptoms of ASD, the underlying disorder had no treatment or cure. My thoughts couldn't help but drift to my schooling days where children with disabilities had had their education far away from those in the general population of a school.

My fear grew, fear that Caylie would cease to be thought of and treated like a person, and just become a statistic—just one more victim of an unexplained disorder. I would fight every step of the way to see that this didn't happen to Caylie. I knew

Caylie would show Dr. Fleisher and the education system that her disability wouldn't define her.

Of course, the fact that school would start again in a few weeks added to my anxiety. Caylie had been so happy at school last year, at least until she walked away and everything had changed. This year, she'd be going back with more severe problems than before.

How would the other teens deal with Caylie's talking to herself? How would the teachers deal with her ups and downs as we tested medications, trying to find the proper dose? What would my parents think of my giving Caylie psychiatric drugs at just fourteen?

The questions were endless.

"I won't allow my daughter to become a zombie with a new medication," I declared.

"I agree," Dr. Fleisher said. "We will only add, change, or remove one medication at a time."

"Look, I'm strong because I need to be. Please, just tell me I'm doing the right thing for my daughter. Not everyone in my life thinks this is the right place for her to be. I need to know for myself, without a doubt, that you and I are doing what's best for my little girl."

"If Caylie had a broken arm, what would you do?"

"I'd take her to urgent care or the emergency room."

"Right."

"So something has caused a misfire in her brain, and bringing her to you is how I can best help her."

"You are doing the right thing for your daughter."

NOT EXACTLY A PICNIC

A s 2017 marched forward, so did the growing number of decisions on Caylie's medical treatment. I was grateful for Dr. Fleisher's patience, as I would ask copious numbers of questions before making the best choice. For me, the worst part of this was hearing all the possible negative side effects and adverse outcomes of the recommended medications.

The logic of doing everything to help Caylie, but possibly hurting her with the wrong medications, felt wrong. But what other options did I have? None could promise me an assured outcome. The only thing I could do was educate myself and make the best possible choices.

In addition to urging me to keep trying to contact the CAN clinic to obtain a testing appointment for Caylie, Dr. Fleisher also provided information about services available to Caylie at the Regional Service Center. In California, the benefits of the Lanterman Developmental Disabilities Services Act of 1969 established the Regional Service Center to help provide support services that would allow those with a disability to live a more independent life. With Caylie's diagnosis of Autism Spectrum

Disorder (ASD), these services would become invaluable for her in the future.

When school got under way, Caylie's treatment seemed to be going in a positive direction despite my apprehension. At home, the construction was complete, and Caylie could fall back into her routine. The primary issue that remained was that Caylie had taken up sleeping in my bed, and I had failed to insist that she return to her bed. With everything Caylie was going through in her young life, I couldn't forcibly take away the security she felt by sharing my massive California King-size bed.

In subsequent visits with Dr. Fleisher, we continued to work on finding the effective medication dosage to help Caylie with her ADHD. While the dosage was working, we soon discovered that Caylie required a supplemental dosage to cover her until bedtime. Adjustments like this helped us make it from day to day, but they felt like maintaining the status quo—holding our own, but making no discernible forward movement.

Trying to contact the Child and Adult Neurodevelopmental Clinic (CAN) had become an endless circle. I had not succeeded in getting testing set up for Caylie, which would enable Dr. Fleisher to have the evidence required to support an autism diagnosis. My leading concern was if the CAN staff couldn't respond to a phone call, why would I think their testing would be of any real quality?

The coming months were a grab-bag of outcomes. Each day with Caylie brought fluctuations in her mood stability and her ability to cope with essential life functions. At the same time, my stress became elevated, as my bills were piling up. Caylie's treatments, my car payments, car insurance, and cell phone showed no leniency. I was thankful for the free room and board at my parents' home. As my parents were aging, I would repay their kindness in working around the house, or taking my mom around town for shopping or appointments.

Time stops for no one, and by October 2017, Caylie had her most successful month since her extreme behavior-changes in March. She was beginning to work on projects and actively participate at school. Although she continued to talk to herself, she was less angry and more positive, and she interacted with other students. Her teacher, Malaka, had helped her set up a fresh-water aquarium at school, and Caylie's grandpa had helped her set up a saltwater tank at home.

The start of the holiday season brought a Pandora's box of moods and new behaviors. We had celebrated Thanksgiving and Christmas day at my grandma's and grandpa's house for years. Since they had passed away, my uncle and aunt now hosted the family holiday. Their house was beautiful for having large gatherings.

There was a formal dining room that always had such elegant red decorations. The staircase had a red and sparkle bow wrapped from top to bottom. The piano sat on one side of the room, and the tree, with delicate decorations, across from the piano. Even a holiday grinch would have enjoyed the effort my aunt and uncle put in.

As with most holidays, the family wandered about, spending time catching up with one another. I ended up chatting with my cousin Melanie. I am the oldest grandchild in our extended family dynamic, and Melanie is the youngest. Growing up, I saw Melanie as a real doll, and I would help Grandma take care of her.

In adulthood, Melanie and I reconnected when Caylie was born. Melanie is a natural-born artist whose work should be in a museum, and Caylie enjoyed visiting Melanie to learn how to make the best paintings. In contrast, Melanie and I couldn't be more opposite when it came to most things. That said, when it came to Caylie, we were both eager to see her healthy again.

"How's Cay doing?" she asked.

"Sometimes things are better than others," I said. "At least here, no one looks at Caylie as if she's crazy when she talks to herself."

I didn't know that I would ever get used to the stares of the general public when I took Caylie out. Some days I handled it better than others. On good days I would smile back as if nothing was wrong, while on the bad days, Caylie and I would stay in the car and wait for my mom to return.

"What do the doctors say we can do to help her?"

"Have patience is usually the top one on the list, closely followed by testing and careful medication adjustment. I can only control the first and last thing. The testing part would require the slightest bit of cooperation with the CAN clinic, and that hasn't happened."

"Do they think therapy would help?"

I'd be lying if I said that I wanted to continue this conversation. I wanted to have any conversation but this one. I could feel my anxiety rising. But I knew that Melanie had good intentions, so I continued to answer her questions.

"She's doing better, Mel, but it's still not exactly a picnic."

"But what about therapy? Therapy helps with mental health."

"I've told the doctor and everybody else, and I'm telling you: it's *not* mental health. I don't know what it is yet, but it's *not* mental health. And if you mean talk therapy, she isn't willing to hold a real conversation with anyone for very long."

"I just think some kind of therapy would help."

"To me, as long as Caylie isn't doing the demon voice anymore, I'm calling it a win."

Sometimes Melanie and I agreed, and sometimes we didn't. In the case of talk therapy, Caylie would not benefit from it right now. I did, however, have it on my list to revisit for Caylie over the coming months.

I again felt so inadequate. I was Caylie's Mom, and I had to trust that I knew I was doing the right thing even if no one else believed it.

In December, Caylie's class had a seasonal gift exchange. I wasn't sure that Caylie even understood what was happening, but I knew that she would enjoy participating with her classmates. Later in the month, we also attended our scheduled appointment with Dr. Fleisher.

"I think she's improved," I told him, "but it's so up and down, it's hard to tell."

"Can you explain what that means?"

"It's like waking up on either the right or wrong side of the bed, but they're in the extremes."

"How are her eating habits?"

"She's eating better and more consistently. I'm trying different things to see if we can get a more balanced diet. But it's a work in progress."

"And how is she sleeping? The last time we spoke, she was still sleeping in your bed."

"She's back in her bed. One positive thing was putting on a movie, and Caylie sat with us to watch it. I can't remember the last time she sat still that long."

"That's an improvement. Were you able to get in touch with the CAN Clinic?"

I was tired of calling and tired of talking about the CAN Clinic. If they were too busy to return my calls, they would be too busy to test my daughter. Although I don't recall the exact wording I used, I know it wasn't positive.

"We need the testing for autism," Dr. Fleisher said, "and their findings are important."

It wasn't until late 2018, almost a year away, that Caylie would finally have formal ASD testing. That testing would be as an inpatient in the Resnick Neuropsychiatric Hospital. Prior to that, I was unable to speak with anyone at the CAN clinic.

We made our appointment with Dr. Fleisher for February, and went to the Dollar Store for Caylie's good behavior shopping reward.

Seeing 2017 come to an end was a huge relief. A new year, a new start, was what we needed. Little did we know that 2018 would stretch our endurance to the maximum.

ACTUALLY, LITERALLY PSYCHOTIC

Caylie stormed down the hallway towards Dr. Fleisher's office, babbling loudly to herself all the way. Her babbling sounded like an entire conversation, except there were no actual sentences, and none of it made sense. Near the end of 2017, I had allowed myself to believe that Caylie was getting better, and more positive times were ahead. In reality, 2018 would be the worst year of our lives.

"Hi, Dr. Fleisher," I said. "How were your holidays and New Year?"

"They were good," he responded. "It's good to see you, and you as well, Caylie."

"It's bullshit! Always bullshit. Liar! She lies." Caylie continued to talk nonstop throughout our whole visit.

"How is Caylie?" Dr. Fleisher asked me.

"Do you even need to ask? Can't you see that things are terrible? Frankly, it's actually a little scary."

"Can you tell me about what Caylie has experienced since her last visit?"

"Thanksgiving was good. And when we got to Christmas,

things were still okay. But after the new year, everything started to fall apart for Caylie."

Dr. Fleisher listened intently to my account of Caylie's return to school in January. It had become increasingly evident that Caylie was living in a world neither her teacher nor I could see. Malaka worked hard to find new and ingenious ways to engage Caylie's interest, but Caylie had slipped beyond anyone's reach. Moments I could identify as reality in Caylie's world had become increasingly rare and farther apart.

"Her teachers say she won't focus or even participate in-class activities," I said.

"*BULLSHIT! LIES! IN ANOTHER PLACE!*"

"I'm sorry, Caylie. But it's true."

"I'll tell Grandma on you. Grandma knows."

"She sits in the classroom and does circles and patterns nonstop," I went on. "Other kids are noticing it. Just what I didn't want to happen."

"How is she sleeping?" Dr. Fleisher asked.

"She's not. No one in the house is sleeping. I know I'm not. She's up all day and all night, pacing back and forth, talking to herself. If I'm late getting home from my part-time job, she won't take her medication from anyone else. I can't quit because I have to pay the bills."

I could barely hear Dr. Fleisher over the noise of Caylie's self-babbling.

"Caylie, I love you, but could you please be quiet long enough that I can hear Dr. Fleisher?"

"Bullshit, won't! Not. No."

"I don't think she can," Dr. Fleisher said in his calm, quiet voice.

"What does that even mean?"

"It's difficult to say."

"Does it mean she's completely broken, so broken that even

you can't help her? That's how I'm feeling right now."

"The first option," Dr. Fleisher said, ignoring my outburst, "is to continue with the new medication and adjust the dosage. But the second option is to reduce and then discontinue the stimulants, as they may be bringing on the psychosis."

If Dr. Fleisher continued talking, I didn't hear it. Even Caylie's consistent chatter seemingly stopped. I knew Caylie's condition had been precarious for the last year. That said, I don't know if anything prepared me to hear that Caylie was now clinically psychotic.

"You just told me my daughter is psychotic, actually, literally psychotic."

"It's difficult at this point to pinpoint the cause of the psychosis."

"All the research and asking you every question I can think of, I still made the wrong decision for Caylie."

"Caylie's condition is complex. Just because this treatment protocol is not working doesn't mean you made the wrong choice. You are doing the best you can."

I would gladly have taken Caylie's place if it meant she could live a happy life. Caylie didn't deserve any of this.

"Why do you think the same stimulants Caylie has taken for years would suddenly start causing psychosis?"

"Since we don't have an exact diagnosis at this point, we need to try adjusting one medication at a time to find improvement."

The way Caylie's treatment plan was starting to develop, I felt that no matter what path we chose, it would be the wrong one.

"So if I understand, we're looking at two maybe's, neither of which promises anything. Please go through this with me one more time. That was a lot of information to process."

I listened to Dr. Fleisher's patient voice explain our options for Caylie one more time. I needed to understand everything clearly so that when school staff or family members asked, I could confidently explain Caylie's treatment plan. Only I knew in reality that I was so far from being confident in anything right now.

Caylie talked nonstop in her meaningless babble during our visit, yet Dr. Fleisher carried on as if this was a usual occurrence. Maybe it was a typical day for him. Like most physicians, they chose a specialization in medical school. Dr. Fleisher had decided to practice psychiatry, and I knew, having researched him, that he had a strong desire to make the lives of his mentally-disturbed young patients better.

"I'm honestly scared," I said. "I'm afraid that when we take away the stimulants, Caylie will become more aggressive."

"We can account for that by increasing one of the medications in her protocol," he said. "We need to be aware of side effects, though, such as weight gain and a decrease in metabolism."

As if things weren't bad enough, there seemed to be nothing good ahead of us. But after fighting for over a year, I didn't plan to let bad news on top of worse news defeat me.

"What else should I be looking for?" I asked.

"Psychosis can be unpredictable," he said. "If Caylie becomes more aggressive or agitated, you need to be prepared to take emergency measures, that is, to take her to the emergency room."

"Then they would call you?"

"She would see the physician on call for the psychiatry department."

"Another doctor who doesn't know Caylie's case. That's a waste of time and effort—for them, for her, and for you."

"It starts a process for possible admittance to the Resnick Neuropsychiatric Hospital. I do visit patients and doctors there."

"But it feels like an unnecessary step on top of other unnecessary steps."

"The process may have some flaws, but it is the process."

While I usually would ultimately support a process, I felt that the patient should be handled by the psychiatry department as soon as possible. People like Caylie deserved to have the least traumatic experience while seeking help. Beyond that, caretakers like me must have effective coordination between a primary doctor, such as Dr. Fleisher, and the hospital psychiatry team.

"Caylie also needs to get labs done. I've already put an order into the system, so if you take Caylie over to the lab now, they'll get them done for her."

"Thank you. When should we schedule our next visit?"

"I'd like to see Caylie in a month. If things change, you can call the desk, and we can move the appointment."

We said goodbye, and left to make the appointment, then headed for the lab.

Caylie's walking pace was five times the speed of mine. Repeatedly, I had to tell her to stop and wait for me, and both of us were frustrated when we finally got to the lab. Once there, it was another forty-five-minute wait.

"Caylie, please sit down," I begged.

"Bullshit! Don't. Can't make us. Me in another world."

I intensely disliked this other world Caylie's mind had created. Or was it our world? I realized, too, how downright bizarre the entire situation had become. After watching Caylie endure nearly a year of blood draws, I hoped she would not give this tech too much trouble. Starting with her angry chatter, Caylie then sobbed uncontrollably in the chair, claiming that they were stealing all of her blood.

But the friendly lab tech gave her some stickers, patted her hand, and told her she was a brave girl. Caylie responded to the kindness and positivity the tech showed her. Someone understood and cared, and I couldn't have been more grateful.

The more Dr. Fleisher had explained Caylie's options, the more discouraged I had become, and the events ahead did nothing to alleviate my apprehension. The following weeks would bring a total implosion of the Caylie we used to know.

NOT A MAGICAL FIX

Our appointment with Dr. Fleisher in late February came with mixed results. Caylie had found it a game to push past Dr. Fleisher to run to his office when he called her name, and Dr. Fleisher didn't mind playing. It was only about a thirty-second walk, but it did allow for some minor Caylie updates without her having to hear.

When we were all in the office, Dr. Fleisher would politely start the meeting off, "It's good to see you, Caylie. How are you doing?"

"Don't want to talk. Don't like it."

"What she meant to say is things keep changing. It's very confusing."

"Can you clarify what is changing?"

"The violent behavior has stopped, which is nice, honestly."

"This is also consistent at school?"

"Yes, they are emailing that she is happier than they have ever seen her. Her teacher is still concerned because she's not trying to do her homework or classwork, but she's no longer causing disruption."

"You said earlier things were confusing; can you clarify that?"

"Caylie has started to do these repetitive behaviors. For

example, if I shower, I tell Caylie where I will be. I also tell her Grandma is downstairs if she needs anything. Then for the entire duration of my shower, no matter how long or short, she opens and closes the outer door. I also asked her teachers about it, and they are noticing the same behaviors at school."

"Would you say the behavior reflects the inability to stop, or does the action stop when you point it out to Caylie?"

"I don't think she can stop. It seems to be on a loop."

Another concern I had for Caylie was the rapid weight gain she had experienced in the last month. It didn't seem like she wanted to stop eating, which was the exact opposite of how Caylie had been before the new medication. When Caylie did talk about it, it was undeniable that she was concerned with being overweight. She would explain to me that her pants didn't fit right, or she would show me that the buttons didn't close.

"I feel like I am giving my kid an eating disorder."

"It is a side effect, and we will need to continue monitoring her weight carefully."

"Yes, but Caylie wasn't an all-star eater before the medication. Now, she's just a terrible eater all the time, instead of sparsely."

As with every visit, we went over the countless options for Caylie, and narrowed it down to one change. I hated and liked this one-change process in equal measure. I felt like things were moving so slowly that every moment was wasting the time Caylie required for school. Yet, this was the way it had to be; otherwise, we had no way to track the change and effect.

With another visit done, we left with more medication. It was hard to look at Caylie because I couldn't imagine what was happening in her head. What had been such a beautiful everyday life for her was now more medications, and everyone treating her with kid gloves. All I wanted for Caylie was a regular life with simple teen things, but that goal seemed to be drifting further and further away.

I would reflect in the quiet moments on how a simple ADHD diagnosis had now become so much more. What did more even mean at this point? Everything was constantly changing, and it seemed like a never-ending journey because Caylie wasn't herself. I was starting to wonder if she would ever be Caylie again, or if this was the new Caylie that I had to begin to understand.

My Caylie, always the sunshine of the family—kind, helpful, cheerful—had now become clumsy, cynical, and mean.

While it was agonizing to decide what medication to trial Caylie on, monitoring her for positive and negative side-effects was critical. It seemed to be a new habit when it started in April: instead of walking beside or around someone, she would bump them hard, and instead of apologizing, she would laugh.

"Caylie, you have to say excuse me, rather than run into people. It's not very nice."

I wasn't sure that Caylie understood, but I had to keep trying to reach her. Beyond the clumsiness, the new medication dosages had brought a constant, endless craving to eat. When she ran out of her snacks at school, she would take other students' food and drinks without their permission.

Needless to say, Caylie was causing a lot of disruption in her class, and problems for her ever-patient teacher, Malaka.

By the middle of April, Caylie's increasingly odd, disruptive behavior at school became too much even for me to justify. She'd started rummaging through trash cans and collecting strange things. When Caylie returned to class with a used feminine napkin, she seemed to have crossed a tolerance line.

Her IEP team had little choice but to recommend that Caylie move to homeschool. Actually, moving Caylie to homeschool was a great kindness by her team. The alternative to homeschooling would have been a suspension.

Of course, homeschooling didn't just affect Caylie; it restructured the whole family's lives, for both my parents and me. My dad was adamant about Caylie getting an education.

"She has a right to go to school," he insisted.

"I am aware of that, Dad, thank you."

"They have to find her a teacher. It's the law."

"I know that, Dad, and they know it, too. But whatever is wrong with Caylie obviously doesn't have a magical fix. Everybody is working on it."

Caylie's IEP support team was doing everything in their power to get Caylie back in school. Unfortunately, the school was limited in its resources for a disability like Caylie's. Finding a new school with available spots would take time and patience.

Meanwhile, Mom chimed in to support Dad's view. "When does she see her doctor?" she demanded.

"In a few days, Mom."

"I'm going with you. That doctor needs to hear what's going on."

"I would say no, but I know it wouldn't do any good."

The April appointment with Dr. Fleisher arrived and found me trying to steer my angry mom and my irrational daughter through the UCLA medical complex. I already had a headache, and we hadn't even made it to the appointment yet.

"Caylie, try not to run into people," I said when she had bumped two people in the hallway of Dr. Fleisher's office building. "If you do bump someone, say 'excuse me, please.'"

"Fine," she snapped.

As he did at each visit, Dr. Fleisher wanted to know how Caylie's life had been going. Unfortunately, the news I brought wasn't good. With Caylie at home full time, I had wanted to help her keep up with her essential schoolwork, such as reading and writing. And I so wanted to have conversations with her. If I couldn't help her, at least I tried to be her voice to Dr. Fleisher and the school, to help them understand what she was experiencing.

But I quickly learned that these hopes would be nearly impossible. Caylie would fight, argue, and throw things rather than even try. I finally realized that this was now her way of communicating. She was telling me how she felt as much as showing me.

These days, Caylie never wore shoes unless forced to do so. On hot days, she wore too much heavy clothing, but too little to stay warm if it was cold. She spent most of her time yelling, pacing, and talking to herself in the backyard.

Mom had listened long enough. "My husband and I don't see any progress with Caylie's treatment."

I love my mom, but I also didn't really want Caylie's doctor to have his head chopped off.

"Mom, Dr. Fleisher is the best doctor Caylie could have."

"Caylie's condition is complex," Dr. Fleisher's calm voice added.

"But Caylie is suspended from school, and she has a right to education. She needs to be at school with other kids. Her treatment isn't helping her do that. Dr. Fleisher, my husband, and I don't think you know what you're doing. We think you've given up on Caylie."

"Mom, out," I said. "Caylie, do you want to go wait with Grandma or stay here with Mommy?"

"Out with Grandma!" she shouted.

When they had left, I apologized to Dr. Fleisher for my mom's remarks. "Please don't give up on my daughter because of my mom," I said.

"She has a right to be upset," he said. "And it's okay for her to express that."

"My parents want me to change doctors, but I won't. And the school keeps asking me what you are doing to help Caylie. I follow everything you recommend to the letter, and Caylie continues to get worse. I think it's time to hospitalize Caylie."

"I don't think we are there yet."

I looked at Dr. Fleisher as if he'd lost his mind.

"Why not? She's body-slamming people and getting kicked out of school."

"There are requirements Caylie would have to meet, such as being a danger to herself or others."

"Since you think I'm wrong, what's the next step?"

Dr. Fleisher realized that Caylie's condition was growing more difficult from every perspective. We agreed to reverse the most recent change in medication and change the medicine that most likely had caused her rapid weight gain. Nothing would be ideal, but Dr. Fleisher's goal, with these changes, was to stabilize her weight and return her to a more functional mental state. Meanwhile, I would try to take one day at a time.

ANOTHER STOLEN BIRTHDAY

May 2018 should have been one of the happiest months of my life. Not only would it be Caylie's fifteenth birthday, but I would graduate with my bachelor's degree in project management. I'd hardly thought about either event. Instead, I'd spent the last several weeks trying to find an educational facility that would accept Caylie as a student and work with her behavioral issues.

My mom, though, had a different plan.

"Misty, we need to book the hotel in San Diego for graduation. It's important."

When I went back to college in 2014, my life had been a much different place than it is now. I worked full-time as a project coordinator under the mentorship of a successful British executive. I had been eager to take my career to the next level through education, which I hoped would provide a stable income for Caylie and me.

All of that changed when my mentor fell ill in early 2015 and left the company a few months later. While I continued through my schooling, I no longer had access to on-the-job experience. Eventually, my position in the company became obsolete, and I left the company with a severance package.

Ironically, having my education would end up helping me manage Caylie's increasingly complex condition. At this moment, I had to come up with something that would appease my mom about graduation, "Mom, I don't see how we can go. Caylie's not doing well, and it's a long drive for you and Dad."

Mom shook her head. "That sounds like a couple of weak excuses to me."

"I've put calls and emails into places where Caylie may be eligible for residential treatment for her behavior issues as well as for schooling. I have to be here so that I get replies from them. Getting Caylie placed back in school is important, too."

"And so is all the work you've put into getting your degree. We are going, and your dad will get to see you receive that diploma. Give me the information about the hotel, please, and thank you."

There comes the point where you know that you are fighting a losing battle. I realized that I would walk at graduation no matter what legitimate excuse I thought up. Like many parents, my degree should belong to them as much as to me. They had gone over the top to make it possible to meet the requirements. We would go, and I would resume the challenge of getting Caylie placed when we returned.

I knew that Caylie wanted to learn, even if she couldn't show it right now. Why was it so hard to get education profession-als and experts in autism to accept my daughter into their programs? My contacts with every facility went something like this:

"Hello." (That's me.) "I need to find out what information you require so that I can complete my daughter's application. Her doctor has suggested that a residential program would be best for her overall treatment."

"I can send you the paperwork." (That's the always friendly, helpful receptionist.) "Once you fill it out, we'll need a letter from her doctor."

"Maybe I should save us both time." (Me again, sounding discouraged.) "I've gone through this about five times. My daughter's case is complex. Whatever is happening with her is now manifesting as a psychosis. As soon as your staff reads her doctor's report, she gets bundled in with mental health. It's not a mental health problem; something else is going on, but we don't know what it is."

"Our residential programs aren't staffed to handle an active case of psychosis. But we would consider cases like your daughter's after a hospitalization. Have you asked her primary doctor if that's an option?"

"Yes, thank you. You've spared me another few hours of paperwork, only to be rejected once again."

How could parents of children who go from being considered within the normal range to a state of psychosis get help? What was I missing?

Finally, graduation weekend arrived. Mom, Dad, Caylie, and I piled into dad's SUV and headed for San Diego. I'd been apprehensive that this would be too much for Caylie. Since Caylie was now homeschooling, we would often stay home, mainly because society still seemed cruel to people who didn't seem to be normal in their eyes.

When we arrived at the hotel, we had dinner and eventually spent time in our room. Caylie and I watched Jeopardy and any animal show we could find. Meanwhile, I knew we would be up early to go to San Diego State University (SDSU), where Ashford University had contracted their graduation.

Caylie barely slept during the night and kept asking me if it was time to get up yet. In the morning, we were both exhausted. Caylie wanted to know everything she would be doing that day. Regardless of how many times I explained the day's routine to her, she would ask again a few minutes later.

In the end, mom had been right. Although the ceremony was long, I have never been more excited to hear my name called. Even with my grandpa's death, my mom's battle with cancer, and now Caylie's illness, I still had managed to earn my degree. I had also decided that I wanted to get my master's degree, and made plans to enroll the next month.

A few days after graduation, Mom and I decided to celebrate Caylie's birthday regardless of her current situation. We wouldn't let another birthday be stolen from Caylie because Dr. Fleisher thought it was autism. I knew better, but I had to find a scientific way to prove it.

Mom and I sang a little 'happy birthday' song, and we cut some cake. I'd bought Caylie some new stuffed animals and colored paints. I wasn't sure that she could even enjoy them now, but at least she'd have them for when she was better.

As Caylie's school came to a close for the quarter, they sent a letter to all parents asking if their student would be attending summer school. Of course, they didn't mean to include Caylie. She wasn't part of the school now. But I responded, asking if Malaka would be teaching. She wasn't, of course. But she did email and ask about Caylie, wishing her a happy birthday. There was no news to give Malaka; nothing had changed, except her getting worse.

Our monthly visit to Dr. Fleisher was brief. The previous medication adjustment had mercifully curtailed the weight gain. It was a substantial but straightforward improvement that could help Caylie feel better about herself. I would always fight for minor improvements because, in my view, Caylie should always feel proud to be who she was, disability or no disability.

"How is Caylie sleeping?" Dr. Fleisher asked.

"She seems to sleep between five and six hours most nights, which probably gives her some quality sleep. But that doesn't mean anyone else in the house is getting any."

"Can you explain why no one else is sleeping well?"

"Someone has to be awake and aware of what Caylie is doing. We sleep in shifts. Caylie is unpredictable, and we're always afraid she'll get up and wander away. You're a parent. If this were your kid, would you be sleeping? No. You'd be knee-deep in books trying to solve their problem. That's where I am."

Caylie had not been on her new medication regime long enough to evaluate its effectiveness, so we had another month ahead to continue the current plan and hope for the best. It would be another month during which Caylie would not be living her life but just existing.

Over the summer, Caylie's condition went from bad to impossibly worse. We missed our late July appointment with Dr. Fleisher, and the first available replacement time was in early September. Whether or not we could hold life together that long, who knew?

WE'RE ON CAYLIE'S SIDE

S ummer in Southern California is one of the best times of the year. The weather is perfect for visiting amusement parks, road trips, or enjoying the beaches. After our last visit with Dr. Fleisher in early July, I wanted to take Caylie on a short trip—anywhere. My hopes of vacation rapidly dwindled as Caylie's overall cognitive state spiraled rapidly downward.

The days when Caylie could function within society became fewer and further between. One of the more challenging moments happened at T.J. Max just before her next appointment with Dr. Fleisher. Caylie, Mom, and I went shopping to get a change of scenery.

I had explained to Caylie that she could only have one stuffed animal on the visit. Although she had repeated it to me before we went in—she could only buy one—she had two when it was time to check out. I asked her to put one back, and Caylie had an outburst. She took to yelling, and swatting at my hands, trying to reach the second stuffed animal.

The hardest part of an invisibility disability outburst is that the cashier was left frightened. While my Mom and I were used to the behaviors, others were not. I was able to get Caylie back to the car while Mom finished checking out.

By the time we reached Caylie's appointment on September 4, I was fighting with my family, Caylie's school, and anyone who dared to become an obstacle in my quest to help my daughter. Caylie saw me as the evil mommy who didn't let her have her way, and she took to throwing things at me, or trying to pull my hair out. While I knew I was strong enough to continue, living on fear and adrenaline takes its toll on physical and mental health.

The drive from home to Dr. Fleisher's office on the UCLA medical campus was horrible. Caylie was angry and antagonistic, and even the wait to see Dr. Fleisher was painfully long. I was exhausted, frustrated, and ready to fight. When Dr. Fleisher finally called our name, Caylie pushed by him, and I just shook my head as we walked back to his office.

"Don't you dare ask me how Caylie is doing. If you can't see it for yourself, I don't know what to tell you."

Caylie had babbled non-stop since we'd arrived, keeping the volume up so that we could hardly talk or hear over it.

"Can you tell me what has been going on?" Dr. Fleisher asked.

Thankfully, Dr. Fleisher couldn't hear my internal monologue about how I'd literally just said not to ask me that question. I knew I wanted to start a fight, because fighting was the only way people listened to me. Instead, I decided to kill him with kindness, or at least the best version I could muster right now.

"Of course. Caylie is no better off today, in 2018, than in 2017 when she first came to see you. By any measure, you and I have made her life worse."

"Caylie's case is complex…"

And that was it! He had gone where angels fear to tread, and had broken the levee.

"Will you stop saying that? It's an old excuse, and I don't want to hear it again! Think up something, anything else to say but that!"

"Based on her age, Caylie's brain is a moving target . . ."

I did try to talk myself into being civil. Caylie was with me in this meeting, and I wanted to set a better example. No matter how much I thought of what to say, nothing came out right.

"Do you know what it's like to have your daughter go missing? If you recall, that's why we started here. Caylie's mind isn't working at all anymore, which means I'm not sleeping. No one in the house is sleeping because Caylie is trying to escape."

"Escape?"

"All Caylie can do is pace. All she wants to do is get out the front door, and walk up and down the street. Two weeks ago, she got out despite all three of us being on watch. She won't wear proper clothing, and will only walk around in socks."

"And what's happening with school?"

"I'm not done yet. As if dressing inappropriately, not wearing shoes, and talking to things that don't exist is not enough, Caylie managed to attack and overpower me. She bit me, clawed me, and drew blood, and it took both my six-foot-two Dad and my six-foot-three brother to get her off me. Do you know how that feels?"

"What about her eating?"

"I'm still not done. My dad wanted to drop her off at the jail and have her locked up. Imagine my very sick child, jailed! That's what happens to children whose moms don't fight as hard and long for them. Then it took both Mom and my brother to talk sense into Dad. He wasn't about to listen to my excuses anymore. My daughter is tearing my family apart, and you keep telling me 'it's complicated.'"

It wasn't complicated to me anymore. My daughter should be in a hospital. It's the one consistent thing I've known all along.

"I need to ask some clarifying questions," Dr. Fleisher said calmly.

"You are going to ask them even if I don't want you to."

"Caylie had been reassigned to homeschooling. Did Caylie go back to school?"

"Yes. The school even gave Caylie one-on-one support, and it was a disaster. Caylie is still a master at getting the upper hand on anyone who gives her an inch. The aid learned that if she was friendly and lenient about anything, Caylie would take advantage of her on everything."

"How has she been eating?"

"Mom made the mistake of getting ice cream. Caylie ate three tubs of it before we realized that no one else was eating any of it. You and I did that. On top of everything else, Dr. Fleisher, you and I gave her an eating disorder."

"Overeating is a side effect. It's very different from an eating disorder."

"Caylie's weight had been stable at 105 for a long time. Then it ballooned with the medicine Caylie was given. I see how it affects her every day, when she doesn't fit into her jeans or dresses anymore. She's devastated."

"Have you been able to get Caylie into the Regional Center?" he asked.

"They sent me the paperwork, but they require both Caylie's and my signature. I can sign for me, but I can't even explain to Caylie why she should do this. Do you see what I'm experiencing?"

"I do."

"All I do is give her pills, and they don't work. Put yourself in my shoes and see what I see day in and day out. She needs to be where she is safe and can get better. She needs to be in the hospital."

"I agree," Dr. Fleisher answered. "It's time for Caylie to be in the hospital."

As Dr. Fleisher looked on in his kindly way, I couldn't hold back the tears. Had I won or lost? On the one hand, I felt like the weight of the world had been taken off my shoulders. On the other hand, I asked that the daughter I loved more than my own life be taken from her small world and confined in a psychiatric hospital.

Deep down, I knew that Dr. Fleisher was, and had always been, on my side, and that both of us were on Caylie's side.

He spoke with the practical information I needed. "You will need to go to the emergency room," he said, "which is just across the street from this building. I will email the hospital to let them know you're coming with Caylie."

"But why can't Caylie just be admitted to the hospital? You're one of their top doctors, and you've been treating Caylie for months. Can't you just order them to admit her?"

"That's not how it works in California," he explained patiently. "The process is that the emergency room has to clear her medically. After that, they call in the consultant for psychiatry to do the psychiatric review. It's the policy and the process."

"Then someone needs to burn the policy and fix the process."

I was making notes on all of the policies that caused additional issues for children and parents. Someday, I would find a way to advocate for improvements. Parents deserved a better process than what Caylie and I were going through.

"I'll walk you out, and please let me know if Caylie gets admitted so I can make adjustments, and I can check in on her."

As I walked with Caylie across the campus drive into another brand-new phase of our lives, exhaustion washed over me. Someone else would keep Caylie safe tonight. Or so I thought.

EMERGENCY ROOM
DOCTORS

welve hours ago, the idea of my fifteen-year-old daughter, Caylie, being admitted to the Resnick Neuropsychiatric Hospital seemed logical. In fact, twelve hours ago, Dr. Carl Fleisher, topflight adolescent psychiatrist, had finally agreed with me that the safest place for Caylie in her present condition was the hospital. Unfortunately, the twelve hours since then had been a nightmare.

Dr. Fleisher had called to let the hospital know we were on the way. Even though Caylie was actively under his care, she still had to be admitted through the emergency room. This extra process adds unnecessary trauma to patients and their families. I didn't like the idea of the process 12 hours ago any more than I enjoyed going through it now.

The emergency room at the Ronald Reagan UCLA Medical Center has two mental health holding rooms where patients in a mental crisis stay until their bed at the hospital is ready. The room had a bed, television, and a locked bathroom. A long desk is outside the wall, divided into rooms where a security guard and nurse watch the patients full-time.

There is a bed for a 3rd patient behind the security guard and nurses' desk, facing the two lockable rooms in the middle room. I imagine that bed is for Alzheimer's patients or less aggressive mental-health patients. The door in that room is to the general ER hallway, and it's locked or closed at all times.

Caylie and I were now in one of the rooms for mental health. It is interesting going through these emotions and conditions with your child. It gave me a unique view of mental health treatment and how someone feels, waiting for the help they need.

The Ronald Reagan UCLA Medical Center where I had sought admission for Caylie is a teaching hospital that, in general, I support as furthering the next generation of medical education. Still, I felt my daughter's case was different than most, and even the highly respected Dr. Fleisher still had not found an effective treatment. I had demanded since Caylie became ill that doctors treat her like a human being, and not a science project.

I decided to hold the ER staff to the highest level, as I did with Dr. Fleisher, to maintain consistency. Caylie's situation had not changed, nor could my expectations of her caregivers. She was a very sick teenager who needed an experienced doctor with the highest possible level of knowledge and judgment.

I was exhausted, and what energy I had left was drained by repeating the same answers to the same questions asked by a nurse, a student, a resident, and the attending doctor. I was having the same conversations over and over. My responses may as well have been recordings.

The attending doctor spoke matter of factly. "Based on the chart, and information you've provided, I'll need to get a consultation with a member of the on-call psychiatric team."

Why, then, wasn't a member of that team talking with us now, instead of a messenger? Sometimes, words hit you in a way that just makes you snap back. I looked at the attending doctor and shook my head. "Then, shouldn't you be doing that now instead of nothing?"

Despite Caylie's choosing to be uncommunicative, the nurses assigned to her were kind, ensuring that she always had water and something to eat if she wanted it. They also made sure she received her current medications on time, and they brought extra blankets for both of us. These enabled Caylie to wrap up like a mummy and watch TV; meanwhile, I could continue working on my laptop after Caylie said she was ready to sleep.

Following my graduation earlier in the year, I'd decided to further my education with a master's degree. Education was the only thing in my life that I felt I could control; and I had homework due the next day. The other benefit to obtaining my master's is that I would have a better understanding of criminal and civil law. I knew that having a degree would force people I came across while advocating for Caylie to see me as more than an average caretaker whom they had to appease.

When I awoke after dozing off over my computer, Caylie was still fast asleep. Scrolling through my text messages, I came across one that seemed familiar. I'd seen it before, more than once. Sprint, my cell phone carrier, would soon be turning off my service. It was a recurring nightmare, a live one that replayed regularly, along with those about car repossession, all adding to my anxiety over future hospital bills. At the same time, I waited for my school stipend to put a slight pause on never-ending bill-collection notices.

My friend Ella had been texting me during the day, and again this evening. I finally told her I would probably stop responding soon. She asked why, of course, and I explained. Ella was a wonderful human being with a strong faith in her God. My faith in anything was weak, which may have been overstating it. I'd concluded that He was paying very little attention to Caylie's needs if a God did exist.

While I was texting with Ella, a Paypal message flashed on, telling me that I had money. I hadn't sold anything recently, and I was puzzled over where the money had come from, as I wasn't expecting it. My transactions list told me. Ella had sent $600, an amount that would cover my phone bill, and allow me to buy some things for Caylie while she remained in the hospital.

I confirmed with Ella that she hadn't made a mistake, and pleaded that I didn't know when I could pay her back. She assured me it wasn't about repayment. I didn't know what to say. I finally managed some kind of 'thank you' and permitted myself to cry.

I had rules about crying. I would never cry in front of Caylie. She required all my positivity and strength to hang on. My crying could frighten her, and I believed she might already be afraid. I refused to cry in front of my family either. I needed to be strong when I explained what doctors had told me to them.

I allowed myself to cry in the dark, in the shower, or anytime I was alone. I could cry if I was angry, scared, stressed, or just feeling sorry for myself. But I would not allow others ever to see a weakness in me.

While Ella's kindness had relieved the despair brought on by the phone emergency, there was no way she could take care of my unfinished homework. It was excruciating finally to send an email to my professor. I described my daughter's current situation, and explained that the rest of my homework would not get done tonight. For the first time in my college career, I had failed to complete my assignments.

A nurse and a security guard were right outside the room assigned to Caylie. The security guard's job was to keep a log of Caylie's behavior, and for ensuring the safety of the nurse and patient in the event of an outburst. The nurse was there to administer medication and watch over Caylie's health.

As Caylie started on this part of her healing journey, it was essential to understand each person's role.

There is an odd silence about this room. It gives you all the time in the world to think without being interrupted. As I lay on the cold floor, I decided to turn Caylie's medical situation into a project. I had a degree in project management, and I would put it to use. Caylie's school, the regional center, social security, and our family would all play roles in the process that was Caylie's current life. All would have questions and would need regular, updated information.

Every time I thought I would doze off, the room would shake much like an earthquake. The room shook around the third time, and I realized a medical helicopter was landing on the roof. I will never know how Caylie managed to sleep through all the noise.

At around midnight, the security guard knocked on the door to let me know that someone from the hospital would be coming to take Caylie up. As with most hospitals, the idea of sleep was illusory. I folded our blankets but kept the pillow with me. The pillow was comfortable, and the nurse said it was mine to keep.

The orderly who came for us had Caylie sit in a wheelchair, holding her belongings. He took us from the emergency room to the Resnick Neuropsychiatric Hospital, Room 4B West. Whole sections of the hospital were empty or in the process of being remolded. It was more than creepy, and I was very grateful for the safe navigation by an orderly.

When we finally arrived at 4B West, we met George, one of the nurses covering the night shift, and another nurse, Lucy, who gave us a packet welcoming us to 4B West. Lucy went through a long list of required questions, and several forms that I would have to sign. Although most of the papers seemed standard, the one that upset me most was about restraints. That brought me to realizing fully how far out of control Caylie's condition had become.

Once I'd completed the questions and paperwork, George took us on a tour of the unit, a large area that seemed a good space for healing. I then saw Caylie's room and met the one-on-one support person who would observe her. A feeling of relief swept over me as I realized that Caylie was finally safe with people who knew how to handle what she was going through.

I said goodnight to Caylie and made my way out of the hospital floor maze. If one thing was for sure, the patients were safe in this part of the hospital. I encountered at least three locked doors before I found what would be the front desk, I thought, during the day.

It was 2:00 a.m. when I left the hospital, and I looked back at the towering building where I had left Caylie. Caylie and I had never been apart for more than two days since she'd been born. Beyond that, Caylie had never stayed anywhere without someone she knew. While I knew the nurses would take care of her, I couldn't help but shed a few tears as I drove home on the 405 freeway.

It was 2:45 a.m. when I made it home. I put the welcome packet to the Resnick Neuropsychiatric Hospital on my desk and would go through it in detail, but it would have to wait until the morning. I was so, so tired. I sent Mom a message that I would sleep until my phone rang and not to wake me early. Finally, I crawled into my bed for the first time in days and was out within seconds.

A LAB EXPERIMENT

There was an unfamiliar stillness in our home in the days that followed Caylie's hospitalization. The chaotic energy that had coursed through every tile and every wall was gone. While there were still three people in the house, the silence was deafening. The house was missing the one person who connected everything … Caylie.

It would take a few days to figure out the routine as it would be until Caylie came home from the hospital. The hospital had strict visiting hours, which were more difficult because of the 405 freeway and its rush-hour traffic. Nevertheless, my Mom and I would go each day to see Caylie and bring her anything from home that she requested.

Caylie's room at the hospital was very comfortable, and nothing like you see in the movies. She had a cute desk, light-brown shelving units, and a single bed. There was also a private bathroom with a shower and bath set-up. We would sit in her room when we visited, and she'd show us any crafts or projects she had completed.

Another thing that became part of my daily routine was a phone-call with Amanda, the hospital resident who would be in charge of Caylie's case throughout her stay. Amanda would call each morning to update me on Caylie's progress, ask for my approval for suggested medication changes, and report on Caylie's treatment plan.

Caylie's teachers and her IEP team helped plan a school routine for Caylie during her hospital stay. While there was the option to place Caylie in the LAUSD (Los Angeles Unified School District) for schooling, I felt that it was critical to stay consistent, with her current team, as she would return to their classes after her hospitalization. The school put together a packet of materials for Caylie to work on, along with the books she would need.

While the items in the packet would never be due for handing in, they would provide a way to keep Caylie learning in a school-like routine. Christina, the school psychologist, became my point of contact to update Caylie's treatment status. There were many moving pieces to getting Caylie healthy, and information needed to flow between them as efficiently as possible.

When Mom and I visited, Caylie seemed slightly better, or, at least, calmer. To me, that felt like progress. But other visits, as well as reports from Amanda, were sometimes discouraging. On one of her calls, Amanda reported that Caylie had softly slapped a nurse trying to apply antibiotic cream to her toe.

"Don't you remember?" I asked Amanda. "I warned you, she hits. You were the one who suggested that she was well enough to be removed from one-on-one supervision."

Although this hitting incident turned out to be an isolated one, it gave Caylie's care team a glimpse of the behaviors that had become all too familiar to me.

Another bump in the road for Caylie's caregivers was getting her to take a shower. Caylie did not like showers: in fact, she hated showers, and threw a fit when anyone tried to force one on her. Caylie loved her long, luxurious bubble baths at home, and the creative nurses found a way to make bubble-baths possible for her at the hospital. When Caylie was happy, life was better for everyone.

While some of our visits were good, there were the other days when Mom and I would arrive, and Caylie would order us to leave, and try to show us the door. She was dismissive of those who wanted most to help her. At times when we were visiting with her, she would wander out into the hall away from us. Typically, we were greeted and showered with profanities.

Amanda, I think, really wanted to be helpful, but at times I found her messages frustrating. Though the medical staff didn't see it this way, to me, it seemed they were trying medications experimentally on Caylie. Every few days, I would approve giving her a new prescription, and, more often than not, the medication wasn't helping Caylie.

I went between frustration and anger because Caylie was not a lab experiment. She was a person who needed and deserved to have a real life. I had repeatedly expressed my feelings about this to Dr. Fleisher, and now it was happening again.

I had learned to appreciate the times my Mom and I arrived when Caylie was at least awake and pacing. At other times we'd find her asleep after medications in the middle of the day. Then I would summon the doctor on duty and clarify that I would not take my daughter home drugged out from her hospital stay. I believed there was always a better way to deal with illness and disturbances.

A regular question nursing staff and doctors always asked: 'Does Caylie enjoy socializing with other people?' Of course, she did—before she got sick and preferred to be in her world on the "other side," rather than in this world.

In her younger school days, not only was she friendly with others, but she reached out to classmates who had unique disabilities. She befriended a child who was deaf and was often alone. Caylie sat by her, drew pictures, and wrote words with her. When an autistic classmate became significantly elevated and upset, Caylie got out the puppets and calmed her down with an entertaining puppet-show.

Caylie always looked for ways to connect with people who needed extra support. But now, those in her age-group weren't doing that for her. Instead, Caylie's behavior would cause peers to avoid her because she could not communicate presently in a way that they understood.

Though I missed Caylie painfully, I knew she was not yet well enough to come home. Doctors began to talk of Caylie's discharge from the hospital. For me, this meant that I'd be receiving a bill and would have to find a way to pay for Caylie's hospitalization. I was grateful that the hospital had a charity I could apply to for the copayment fees. I believed, and strongly hoped, that we would qualify for it.

The implications of Caylie's returning home were formidable. Caylie's being at home would also mean getting her back into school. But that wasn't the factor that ended the move to discharge Caylie.

Discussing the patient's medications with the patient and the family was essential for the discharge process. I had discussed Caylie's medicines with the doctor, and we had agreed that keeping her hormones stable might help her overall condition. But when a nurse explained it to Caylie, she thought the nurse meant that she was pregnant.

Confused and upset, Caylie began to cry, hitting me, and threatening to hit my Mom. The staff could clearly see that Caylie's emotional stability and self-control were not ready for the ups and downs of family life. The discharge was off.

I wish I could say that I was immune to the frustration and annoyance that came with some elements of Caylie's hospital stay, but I was not. As my level of frustration rose with each day, Caylie's rose also. I found it painful when Caylie persisted in showing us the door each time Mom and I visited. It hurt in a different way when I had to borrow money from family members or my friend Ella just to park in the hospital parking lot.

I could see that Caylie was tired of being in the hospital and wanted to be at home. On a good day, she would proudly show us her projects and other items she had worked on in her classes. Meanwhile, her daily journal showed how much she missed home and hated being in the hospital. We expressed our frustrations differently, but I understood what she was feeling.

Before long, preparation for her discharge began again. The social worker gave me information about the regional center, but the center had been so hard to contact before that I couldn't expect much help. However, I would try again for Caylie's sake.

Meanwhile, I had rearranged Caylie's room at home, and made it more spacious by removing the clutter of things she'd been hoarding. She would have a fresh start as she resumed her teenage life. I was laying the foundation that I hoped would be successful for Caylie.

I was apprehensive and angry at the discharge meeting. Though Caylie was coming home, she still wasn't herself. The doctor and the hospital staff took the easy way out and settled for the autism label. However, there was no testing, nor anything provided to support the diagnosis.

I read the master plan the staff provided me with, and did my best to ask thoughtful questions, but nothing made sense. After a month of hospitalization, Caylie was, indeed, leaving less angry—but so heavily medicated that I didn't consider it a win. Unless something changed, I knew my sweet girl would be back in the hospital before long.

WE WERE TREADING WATER

aylie was excited to explore her re-decorated room. She'd completed many arts and crafts projects at the hospital, and wanted to display them there in her new space. Caylie's passion for art had grown, and some of the more memorable moments were when she would talk to me about it. Caylie would color in her new coloring books, and tell me why she'd picked the colors for the image.

While things seemed better for Cay, I was concerned about how the new medication protocol affected her. I knew that Caylie was living in a fog, where sometimes she'd enjoy a few hours out of every day. For the moment, it was a stable fog, but she wasn't living; she was simply existing.

Caylie spent hours pacing, or sitting on the bench swing in the backyard. When I would join her, she would tell me how warm the sun was or about the trees. She didn't say very much if I asked her how she felt. There had to be a better solution to help Caylie; I just had to find it.

Just as during the hospital stay, bubble baths and bath bombs saved many days. They could make a distraught Caylie into a happy one, which made all of us happy too. Making her bubbles and then floating around in them were the magic times of Caylie's day.

After a lengthy hospital stay such as Caylie's, the key to success is rooted in follow-up and aftercare. The social worker at the hospital had scheduled two appointments with Dr. Fleisher and one with Caylie's general physician, and had contacted the school to schedule an IEP. Getting through these appointments would be the first challenge Caylie would encounter after her hospital stay.

Meanwhile, Christina, the school psychologist, had begun investigating educational opportunities tailored explicitly to Caylie's needs. The one thing I knew would be necessary for Caylie's recovery was adequately-trained and dedicated teachers. Christina took the time to examine the possibilities, and planned for us to make visits in early November.

The staff at Caylie's school, including her IEP team, never gave up on her. They checked on her regularly, and we always knew we had a support team for Caylie. I had come to terms with Caylie leaving the school to better support her education, but it would be difficult to leave the team we'd built there.

Around this time, I met Marie Pierre, the Director of Student Support at Caylie's school. Marie was about 5'7", with dark, beautiful, black skin, and curls that fell about her face in tight ringlets. I wish I could say by this point that I had learned to trust new people along Caylie's journey, but I hadn't. Luckily for me, Marie was determined to help me, and we met for breakfast at Eggs N' Things.

Marie wanted to help me get Caylie's paperwork organized, introduce me to the Family Focus Resource Center, and ensure that the regional center benefits were accessible to Caylie. After breakfast, Marie and I drove over to the family focus center. I was in awe of all the books, binders, and information that was now within my reach.

That day, the woman running the center provided me with a binder to organize Caylie's paperwork. Tears threatened to spill from my eyes, but I felt that I would recapture control of Caylie's medical journey by creating this binder of records. Marie drove us back to get my car from Eggs N' Things, and asked me to forward the information from the regional center.

As we arrived back at my car, Marie and I hugged. I had made a new friend, someone who wanted to teach me how to handle complex government agencies. We also exchanged phone numbers, and Marie advised me to call if I required help with any agency. On the drive home, wondering how I was so lucky, I knew that Caylie's school team wanted nothing but success for her.

On our first post-hospital visit to Dr. Fleisher, Caylie went without so much as a protest. In general, her previous visits had been exhausting for everyone. Caylie always sat in the back right seat, and on the drive to UCLA that day, she would look out of the window, and sometimes I saw her singing with the music.

The ease of going to a doctor's visit came as a relief. My Mom was also in the car, as she had decided to go with us. Mom wanted to know what Dr. Fleisher would say about Caylie's current condition. Everyone at home believed Caylie was at least fifty percent better, but I was still concerned about her medications and their side effects.

Though I worried about Caylie's constant pacing, believing she should be doing something more constructive, Dr. Fleisher explained that pacing was likely the way she regulated herself. In my view, he was explaining away a condition, while I was concerned about the person experiencing it. Dr. Fleisher wasn't the one who took care of her feet after hours of pacing, or watched her sitting in the swing, staring endlessly at the sky.

My beautiful Caylie had danced and sung, picked flowers, looked for the most beautiful leaves on the trees, and presented me with the most unique-looking rocks. Where had the magnificent wonder that Caylie had shown me all these years gone? I refused to believe that everything that made Caylie so uniquely amazing would never return. Even now, after everything we'd been through, I would have enough hope for both of us.

During Caylie's second post-hospital visit, Dr. Fleisher again advised me to follow up with the regional center. At the same time, the regional center seemed bent on denying benefits to Caylie. Their staff believed that Caylie's conditions and needs were not factors they could support. Meanwhile, Dr. Fleisher continued to adjust Caylie's medications, and I felt that we were treading water.

Between the first and second visits with Dr. Fleisher, Caylie's aggression became a significant issue. It was starting to feel like *deja vu* when it came to what Caylie was experiencing. Previously, medication to control aggression had brought on Caylie's uncontrollable appetite, which resulted in emotionally-devastating weight gain.

"How can I keep giving my daughter medication to counter the side effects of other medication?" I asked. "She takes so many pills, and yet she remains mad at the world."

"Medications can have long-term effects that work toward progress," Dr. Fleisher responded. "It will take time to find the right medications for Caylie."

"How many times are we going to do this song and dance?" I asked. "How long should my daughter be used as a UCLA test subject? She's a kid who should be enjoying her life, and instead, she's a glorified lab rat. I want her to live life to the fullest extent of her abilities."

I was starting to feel like a broken record.

In his calm, professional manner, Dr. Fleisher explained it all again. There would almost always be a delay in seeing therapeutic changes with Caylie's medications. Most medications we were trying required at least two weeks for noticeable changes, but some would need up to three months.

Caylie had already been waiting this long for something to work: what was the real difference? I knew that Dr. Fleisher was doing everything in a way that should have resulted in Caylie's healing, but we hadn't found the correct protocol for Caylie. It broke my heart to tell Dr. Fleisher that Caylie was physically there with us, but the light was out, and no one was home.

We made adjustments to Caylie's medication, and set an appointment to return. I tried to ask Caylie what she was thinking, but she never allowed me inside. I continued to hope that whatever part of her that might remain from the beautiful, happy child she had once been would stay safe and be patient. I would never stop fighting to find it.

I WAS WRONG

We were now twenty months into doctors and hospitals. The holiday season's approaching was a stark reminder that Caylie's condition was worse now than it had been last year. I would keep fighting to find answers for Caylie. I had to believe that this was just another bump in the long, twisted journey we were on.

By November 2018, Caylie's behavior was again rapidly deteriorating, and if she wasn't slapping or biting, she was obsessively repeating actions that kept everyone on edge. Once a week, my cousin Melanie would take Caylie over to my aunt and uncle's house. Melanie would either work with Caylie on speaking French or teach her to make muffins or brownies.

I invited Melanie to join the IEP team, as we required Caylie to have some measurable schoolwork for the fall report card. Caylie had rejected my attempts to teach her, and Melanie offered to try. Melanie recorded Caylie slowly speaking French, and reported that Caylie showed some willingness to stir the muffin batter. It wasn't much, but it was enough for the report card.

The formal IEP was one of the most challenging moments of my life. While the teachers and others gave ideas for Caylie's goals and current educational progress, the whole meeting for me was a strain. I wish I could say I was optimistic that Caylie was ever going to meet the very simplistic goals we set, but I wasn't.

I selfishly wanted a break from all the demands I felt creeping in around me. There was a growing list of things I needed to follow up on to make progress for Caylie. I knew that life doesn't stop for self-doubt or self-pity, and that I needed to persevere.

Christina, Caylie's school psychologist, approached me with a live-in educational facility to meet Caylie's current academic needs. In truth, I had forgotten about the possibility of a live-in facility for Caylie. The last thing Caylie should require is schooling away from her family support. Regardless, I had to be open to the possibility even if I disliked it.

Christina had arranged a facility tour of a program that would accept Caylie with her special medical and psychiatric conditions. I also invited Victor from Caylie's IEP team to tour the school. Victor had been Caylie's IEP coordinator in the 7th and 8th grades. He also knew Caylie before she had the regression she was experiencing now.

With everything I was keeping track of, I felt that having Victor as an extra set of eyes would be helpful for me. Already I didn't particularly appreciate that this school was on a busy street. I had lost count of the car horns honking, and the sirens of emergency vehicles we heard before pulling into the parking lot.

When Caylie and I arrived at the building, it reminded me of a nursery school. We walked through the small parking lot and rang the doorbell to the building. As we entered, the door buzzed and locked behind us. The buzzing sound followed by the clicking lock happened at each exit we passed through.

I found this disturbing. I realized that increased safety was necessary for a facility that dealt with autism and all kinds of emotional disabilities, but school should not be like a prison.

Caylie deserved a space that would be more personal, and warmer.

We were glad when the tour was over. Christina and Victor agreed that this was not the school for Caylie. I did try to include Caylie by asking her thoughts on going to the school, but she wasn't interested in having the conversation. As disappointing as it was, Christina decided to expand her search to include facilities farther away. I reluctantly gave the okay, but I required Caylie to come home on weekends.

The decision-making about Caylie seemed endless. I had decided to entrust her well-being to Dr. Fleisher, and he had been unable to resolve her issues. Her residency as a patient at Resnick had worked for a month, only long enough for her to return to Dr. Fleisher. Now it would be up to me, the person who loved her most, to send her away from the only home she had ever known to continue her education. But before that could even be a possibility, a still bumpier road lay ahead of us.

In these twenty months of Caylie's challenging journey, I had learned to keep my emotions separate from the logical, evidence-based decisions I had to make. Over the next few days, the fragile construct I had built to support my sense of control collapsed. For the first time since all this began, I could no longer see glimpses of my Caylie, the sweet, loving little girl who used to dance, sing, and help me in the garden.

I had started implementing the changes required to Caylie's medication, as Dr. Fleisher had advised at our last appointment. Tiering her dosages down would help determine what was or wasn't working. While I had heard this at other times, I still believed it could work. This time, though, Caylie's behavior became unmanageable.

One of the many changes to the house during the remodel was installing a walk-in disability bathtub. Caylie required extra support to wash her hair and shave, which had never been a big deal in the past. I didn't expect anything to change.

I was wrong.

I went through the motions to wash Caylie's hair, and this time Caylie took offense and grabbed my wrists. I tried to pull them away from her, and an awkward struggle began. When she started trying to break my fingers, I panicked, finally managing to get one hand free while she bit at the other hand and clawed my face.

I was terrified of my own daughter.

Everything that could go wrong, did. My glasses crashed to the floor and broke, and Caylie started punching my face and digging her nails into my arms. I was bleeding, couldn't see, and was painfully hurt physically and emotionally.

Eventually, I finally managed to push her head back to break her bite on my arm and put distance between us.

"Caylie, we don't hurt people," I said.

"You deserved it," she responded.

"I need you to drain the tub and dry off," I managed.

With the water drained, she'd be safe to get out, and I had to get away.

I went upstairs to hide and cry in my room. I also needed to figure out what required cleaning and bandaging. My right arm had five deep claw marks, and my eye would have a bruise, but I could move all ten fingers. That seemed like a good thing.

I glued my glasses back together so that I could see, then sat on the floor of my room and sobbed. All the anger, frustration, and pressure I'd been holding in hit me like a ton of bricks. My heart had shattered into a million pieces, and no glue, I believed then, could ever put it together again.

Crying wouldn't solve anything, and seeing my weakness could encourage Caylie's aggression. I had to think and act. Caylie's aggression was far from an ordinary daily incident.

Caylie's behavior had risen to a different level, the emergency level. I had to get up, get myself together, and take the emergency action advised by Dr. Fleisher. Emergency action meant contacting Dr. Fleisher's office, taking Caylie in for him to evaluate, reaching out to the hospital, and, once again, the emergency room and hospitalization. It was time.

When I ventured downstairs to tell my parents Caylie had to return to the hospital, I expected they would agree and be sympathetic. Instead, they were not at all supportive. Mom sided with Caylie and Dad; he was never fond of hospitals anyways.

"You can't just send her away," she said. "This is her home, and we love her."

"I love her, too, Mom, but she's sick. She's hitting herself and injuring me. I have to act to stop it and help her. I can't let her keep on like this."

My Dad went down the road of genetics again, "Do we know she doesn't have Tourette's like your cousin did? I think it's probable."

Did I think it was Tourette's Syndrome? No. Did I think the doctors were missing something in Caylie's genes? Yes. I had to find someone to order the genetic testing. Maybe there was something, or maybe there wasn't, but until we had facts, I wouldn't rule anything out.

"Dad, I asked, and they ruled out Tourette's. That's not what Caylie has."

"Well, if you want to do wrong, do it yourself. Caylie will learn to hate you forever if you keep doing this. I'm not going with you to lock her away."

"I know, Mom. I can live with being hated for trying to help."

There was no win to be had. Whatever I did would be painful to me as well as to Caylie. My Mom might have been harsh, but she was acting out of love for Caylie, and I think I knew that somewhere. But Caylie had forced my hand with her aggression, and I had to act in her best interest and for her safety.

I decided to pack Caylie's bag, and with Caylie's angry mood, things went flying here and there. It was late, and no one was happy. I went through the motions of getting Caylie into the car, and I prepared to drive.

Instead, I just sat in the driveway. Caylie was sobbing in the backseat, and I knew I shouldn't be going anywhere while the situation was this emotionally charged. Nothing would change between tonight and early in the morning. Caylie and I went back into the house, and we would face this again after a few hours of sleep.

The following morning, I talked with Melanie, who had sided with Mom and disagreed with my returning Caylie to the hospital. I felt totally alone, and the anxiety was too much; I could hear my heart racing, and I wanted to scream. I missed my Grandma. If she were here, none of this would be happening. She would have told everyone Caylie needed help.

My Grandma was a remarkable woman. Beyond raising her own four boys, she helped raise six of her eight grandchildren and then Caylie, her great-granddaughter, for seven beautiful years. My Grandma took great pride in driving disabled youths to school in our valley for over 30 years. I believed that all she'd taught me about having a disability prepared me for this uphill battle to help Caylie.

After my lackluster conversation with Melanie, I called Dr. Fleisher's office and secured an appointment. Caylie started the day unhappily, and when I picked up Melanie, she still didn't like the idea. Meanwhile, I had to do what I felt was right, no matter how hard it was.

With Caylie talking to herself all the way and Melanie angry with me, the ride was miserable. I did try to have some conversation, but it all turned into an argument. Why couldn't people just trust in me to do the right thing? Or, at the very least, give me the benefit of the doubt.

When we finally arrived at Dr. Fleisher's office suite, Caylie moved by the person who opened the door to the offices. She was headed straight to the middle room between the waiting room and Dr. Fleisher's office. The room had a dollhouse, some crayons, and chairs. Caylie liked to play there, and having her contented made my time more manageable. It wasn't the actual waiting room, but it was at least close enough.

Before long, Dr. Fleisher called us into his office. While Dr. Fleisher went through his question routine as per usual, as soon as I started to explain our being there to Dr. Fleisher, Caylie ran to the door. I had reached the limit of my patience with everyone and everything.

"No one is leaving this room until we all agree on something!" I ordered.

Dr. Fleisher had always remained calm and collected no matter what happened. At the moment, I resented it. "No one," he responded, calmly but authoritatively," No one has to stay in the room."

I took his words as a reprimand and, with my face in my hands, went to my chair. Melanie chased Caylie down the hall while I just shook my head and cried. "You can't understand," I said through my sobs.

"Nothing about this is okay. Any decision I make has potential consequences. Nothing I do makes things better. If I do something I think is right for Caylie, and Mom disagrees, she will threaten to kick me out. I know Mom might not mean it, but it's exhausting. My cousin takes Mom's side against me, too."

Dr. Fleisher had been listening intently. "You came here

today because you need me to tell your cousin that hospital-ization is the right thing for Caylie, right?"

"I sent you the email."

"Then let me talk to your cousin. You sit with Caylie. Let me help you so that you can help Caylie."

Finally, someone had made sense, and it was Dr. Fleisher. I went into the hallway to oversee Caylie. She wasn't happy about it, and frankly, at the moment, neither was I. It was clear to me now how far beyond reality Caylie had gone, and I was dealing with what remained.

I'd thought I could take Caylie straight to the emergency room from Dr. Fleisher's office. However, a typical family conflict came up and had to be resolved, not about Caylie, but about getting Melanie back home in time for her school commitments. That meant I'd have to drive two hours each way to get her home before I could take Caylie to the emergency room and begin the arduous hospitalization process.

Finally, an angry Caylie and I were there at 8 p.m. It wasn't long before Caylie took a swing at me, and a security guard was assigned to us right away. It had been a day from hell.

DO NO HARM!

U nlike in Caylie's September hospitalization, the mental-health rooms in the Emergency Room (ER) were completely full. Caylie and a young man were assigned beds in the hallway, just outside the mental health rooms. The less than desirable layout meant that all five mental-health patients shared the same nurse, with two security guards also covering all five patients.

Even with more patients, it seemed that the waiting time to see a doctor was moving more quickly than it had in the past. There were either process improvements, or whoever was running the floor was more effective. Regardless, the attending doctor came by to see Caylie, accompanied by a resident doctor.

The attending doctor explained that his resident would be recording the notes while he completed the preliminary workup. The two doctors working together felt more productive than the last visit had, which in my view was better for everyone. As I expected, both doctors wanted to know what medications Caylie was currently taking.

Caylie and I took her medication bag everywhere, and a hospital visit was no different. The doctors took detailed notes of Caylie's current medications and others that weren't successful. Much like before, the ER doctors would need to call in a consult with the on-call psychiatric team. However, before they left, I made it clear that Caylie had to be given her medications on time.

Over the last two years, I had learned through trial and error that it was essential to give Caylie's medications on time. If I were late with medications, Caylie would become frustrated or angry. While it wasn't perfect, I had adjusted my Lyft driving schedule to ensure that I was always home at Cáylie's bedtime. I did not doubt that the ER staff was well versed in giving medications on time.

Meanwhile, we had missed the dinner serving time at the hospital, and Caylie was hungry. A kind nurse brought her crackers, which immediately became missiles for Caylie to throw at me. I couldn't decide if it was funny or serious, but the security guard ordered her to knock it off. Shortly afterward, the nurses relocated Caylie's bed into one of the mental health rooms that had now opened up.

When the resident doctor of psychiatry came in for her consult, we went through all the usual questions. I then handed her all the medications I'd brought in my bag, except for one day's supply that I'd held back for an emergency. She found it humorous that I was a walking pharmacy and had extensive knowledge of what every medication did, and when Caylie required each dose.

I sat on the cold floor, waiting for a bed at the hospital to be available for Caylie. My eyes wandered to the clock, and I felt my anxiety rising. The doctors and nurses knew that Caylie required her medication at 7:00 p.m., and time was ticking well past 8:00 p.m. No one seemed to understand that Caylie was a ticking time bomb, and the only way to defuse her was to provide her medication.

I stepped outside the room to ask a nurse where Caylie's medications were, and Caylie, frightened and annoyed, followed me out. The security guard stepped forward and told Caylie abruptly to get back in her room. Instead, she dashed to escape, and the guard radioed for backup. So a 250-pound guard needed backup to handle a 135-pound teenager. What exactly was the backup going to do in this situation?

"I told you this would happen!" I yelled to the nurse and guards. "Caylie needs her medicine!"

How was this evening happening?

Caylie was now struggling with both guards. "Let me go!" she screamed.

There was something about Caylie's scream that rattled me to the bone. I could hear the blood rushing through my ears. I was trying to ground myself in meditation because I was about to faint. I could see the room spinning, and this was the very last thing that could happen right now. I had to be Caylie's voice.

"You need to calm down," her assigned guard answered. "If you don't, we'll have to restrain you."

"Like hell, you will do anything such thing!"

Now, I was angry. If there was one sure thing to make the world stop spinning, it was a threat to my sick daughter. With two grown men holding her down, Caylie screamed at the top of her lungs.

I moved over by Caylie, put my arm behind her back, laid my head gently on hers, and ran my fingers through her hair. "Come on, baby," I said softly. "I need you to calm down. We can do this together, but I need you to calm down."

"I wanna go home. I wanna home!"

Caylie was nearly beyond reason, trying to struggle with

these guards. Her chest heaved, and she was almost choking on her breath. Where the hell were the nurses or doctors? To hell with the security guards!

"I know, baby. Can you just breathe? Please just take a breath. Can you let Mommy go and see what she can do? Can you do that for me?"

Everyone started to let go of Caylie. Gradually, she became calm, and her muscles relaxed as she sobbed.

I reached for the medicine bag. "Caylie," I said, "Mommy will be right back. Can you be brave for a few minutes while I go and get you some help?"

"I'll be right here."

Just outside Caylie's room, more security guards had gathered along with a nurse and a doctor. It was time for some people management, time for me to take charge because this was never happening again.

"Which one of you overpaid people is this kid's doctor?" I asked.
"Ms. Wolf . . ."

"I told you the exact time Caylie required her medication."
"Ms. Wolf.."

"Yet the nurse, there, didn't have an order from you, and Caylie has not had her essential medication. You have failed at your one job! So here's my plan, and you have no say, so shut up and listen. I'm going to sit down right here and put her nighttime meds together . . ."

Now it was the security guards manager who decided to chime in. He had no idea how big a mistake he had just made.

"Ms. Wolf, we normally . . ."

"Mr. Security Guard, spare me what you're about to say. I know you typically lock up medication. But the fact is, people around here sometimes don't do their jobs. Frankly, that is in spite of the fact that other people's lives depend on them.

That's why I carry all Caylie's meds in this bag—because our lives have come to rely on this bag. It's what makes me the supermom who solves the crisis when doctors forget how to do their jobs. Today is a glowing example of what the consequences are when that happens."

"You have Caylie's medications, Ms. Wolf?" the nurse asked?

"I do."

It's not my policy to yell at nurses. Sometimes they're all we have to keep us alive when doctors are exhausted, and security guards are over-zealous.

I could barely hear the doctor standing behind the nurses and guards as he spoke, authorizing me to give Caylie her medication. It was a formality; Caylie was getting her medication with or without the doctor. He's already failed her once: that wasn't happening again on my watch.

"Now, I hope you will all remember that when a family member tells you a patient needs their medication, it's not a joke . . ."

"Ms. Wolf . . ."

"I have a right to be angry. My young daughter followed me into the hall because she was frightened and wanted to stay close to her Mommy. Then, you had insane security guards tackle her to her bed like this is football instead of a place of healing. Three grown men, easily over 800 pounds in total if not more, held her down and terrified her even more because you were too busy to order her medicine. You're a doctor! Commanded by your oath to do no harm! Remember this moment, and do better next time for some other kid."

I had made my point. I turned on my heel and went back into Caylie's room. Thankfully, the nurse provided me with a water pitcher, and Caylie quickly took her medication. I petted Caylie's hair until she was fast asleep.

The rest of the evening was relatively uneventful. There was not a peep from anyone until about 12:30 a.m. The security guard advised me Caylie's bed was ready, and an orderly would be here shortly. Unfortunately, there was no way to move Caylie without waking her up, which put her into overdrive again.

Once out of the ER and in her hospital room, though, she was able to relax again, and sleep, and I was able to get the paperwork done to sign her in. It was seemingly faster than the last time I had checked Caylie in here. Leaving her here would never get easier, but I had to trust the nurses, doctor, and security guards to take care of her.

I made my way down to pay my ransom to exit the parking area. Paying the parking fee once or twice a month for visits to Dr. Fleisher was one thing, but paying it every day while Caylie was a resident patient was another. Finally heading away, leaving an exhausting day behind, I barely remembered the family drama earlier in the day.

The nineties music on my radio made me feel better as tears ran down my face. At 1:30 a.m., I didn't care if I was still unwelcome at home. I had a key, and the additional hours to Ella's place were simply not physically possible in my current state. Later, Mom would tell me she'd left messages telling me Dad had said he was wrong. But Caylie had needed every bit of my energy, and I hadn't been paying attention to messages. Sometimes distance helps clarify things on both sides, and this time it definitely did.

After all, I'd been through with Caylie; I couldn't think about the approaching holidays. All we'd done over the last three months had been for nothing: we were right back where we'd been last time she'd entered the hospital. I'd told them when they discharged her before that nothing had changed—she'd be coming right back. I was right. I knew my daughter better than they did.

When Caylie's new doctor, Linda, called to introduce herself, I answered the same questions I'd been asked so many times before. The questions were always the same, though sometimes in a different order. The one thing I told Dr. Linda I wanted was genetic testing. The number of people with medical degrees who had been unable to offer any real progress for Caylie was long, and growing. My gut feeling was that it was something in the genetics that everyone was missing.

Dr. Linda's response was the most encouraging news I'd had in a long time. She advised that it was protocol to conduct genetic testing on an ASD patient during the second hospitalization, with the parents' consent. At least that was one less thing I would have to fight with the doctors to obtain.

HOME VIDEOS

As the hospital was willing to do genetic testing, I had a brief conversation with Caylie's father. We both agreed that we would do everything in our power to ensure that Caylie's health improved. It would be one step closer to finding solutions to Caylie's mental and behavioral difficulties.

The genetic testing would require a blood sample from Caylie, her father, and me. From there, it would go to the genetics lab at UCLA, where it would take six to eight weeks for the results. At that point, we would know if Caylie had extra or duplicated genes, or if any of her genes had a substantial variant.

In the first week of hospital updates, Dr. Linda dealt primarily with medication adjustments, testing plans, and Caylie's day-to-day activities. Caylie also had the blood draw for the standard hospital-stay tests and the genetic testing. Otherwise, the first week did not have any positive updates.

Caylie knew she was in the hospital because I had put her there. She was confused, and walked around the floor endlessly. When a staff person wanted her to do something she didn't want to do, she'd ask to take a bath. She was doing what she'd be doing at home, though the medication was tempering her aggression in the hospital.

While Caylie focused on getting well, the search for a school for her continued. Christina, the school psychologist, had found a placement for Caylie in our local school district. The teachers in the moderate-to-severe program were both educated and experienced in complex disabilities.

Christina was dealing with her own health issues, but she remained determined to ensure that Caylie had a school to return to after the hospitalization. The entire IEP deserves credit. They went above and beyond, even in the most frustrating of circumstances.

In my downtime, I managed to power through my own school assignments. These were the only times I could dedicate entirely to myself. Between the minor in civil and criminal law earned in my BA degree, and my degree-in-progress in criminal law, specializing in forensics, I planned to be the best advocate Caylie could have.

My Grandma had taught me that when I needed to know something, I should pick up a book and learn it. I picked up books and studied law, disability services, and how to pursue goals that would help Caylie succeed. I would soon have the education to make me a formidable advocate for Caylie instead of just another stay-at-home mom whom they could push around.

Despite Mom's and my own arguments against it, Dad wanted the household to set up a Christmas tree. Caylie was the one who loved decorating a tree, reveling in the happy colors and lights, and being the sparkle in so many lives. To me, if there was no child, there was no tree.

In addition to Doctor Linda's calls, I also received regular calls from Danielle, Caylie's hospital caseworker. Danielle always took the time to listen to my concerns, and she read through all the documents I sent her. Danielle had become a welcome change to the hospital social worker Caylie had had during her first stay. I felt that Danielle wanted to see Caylie thrive after her release, which was the most important thing to me.

To ensure a successful transition back home, Danielle assembled her team to meet with me, Mom, and Caylie. I prepared videos of Caylie when she was younger, and IEPs from before her regression. I wanted this team to know the real Caylie and her story: then, maybe, they would come up with a better approach to helping her.

The big surprise to Danielle's team was that Caylie had been so verbal in the past. The home videos that I provided to the team were a stark contrast to the Caylie they had seen during her hospital stays. While in the hospital, Caylie would say only a minimum number of words. Now they knew that Caylie had once been a different person. To make the meeting even more productive for me, a staff person provided me with two sets of paperwork for genetic testing: one for me, and one for Caylie's father.

During her second week in the hospital, Caylie began asking to go home, and calling the hospital a dungeon. She hadn't lost her humorous way of naming things. I wanted her home and healthy more than anything in the world. But all I could do was call, visit, and make the best decisions presented to me. Caylie wasn't well enough to come home yet.

In the middle of Caylie's second hospital week, her handwashing behavior became repetitive. At first, I thought she was just worried about keeping them clean. However, her hands were very chapped, and becoming raw by the following week. The nursing staff was applying lotion to them, but the obsessive behavior had me concerned.

In mid-December, Danielle called and wanted to set up a meeting to prepare for discharge. We'd been here before, talking discharge when it wasn't clear that Caylie was ready. I would listen, but I had questions that the doctors would need to address. I had to know what to expect for Caylie when she came home.

During the week, Caylie had started to call home, telling me about her day and describing what she had done. She was calm, no yelling, no expletives, just Caylie's clear voice expressing clear thoughts and feelings. I couldn't remember when I'd been so happy to see a UCLA number on my phone.

When we arrived at the meeting, I gave Caylie a book I'd brought, one I knew she loved. She rushed down the hall, excited and smiling, to take the book to her room. Her smile made me teary. It wasn't a fake smile, but one I hadn't seen since our ordeal started. Her beautiful blue eyes were alive again, and she was actively enjoying her life.

For the first time, when Mom, Danielle, and I sat down to talk about Caylie, I felt there was hope. First, we'd received confirmation that Caylie's genetic testing, along with mine and her father's, had been received and processed by the Resnick Neuropsychiatric Molecular Diagnostics labs. However, the results and interpretation would not be available for two or three months.

Danielle reviewed all the information she had assembled, and discussed points in Caylie's medical and IEP history, which could have indicated autism or ADHD all along. She talked to me, not at me, and made me feel empowered by the information rather than threatened by it.

Another hopeful indication was Danielle's advice to get an IEP meeting arranged. To me, though, the most important thing that was happening was getting Caylie back home in time for Christmas. That was the best gift anyone could give us.

December 20 was finally the day Caylie would come home. Danielle's reports on Caylie being so happy to go home were fantastic. Dr. Linda said that Caylie understood that the medications made her feel good, and she knew she was going home Friday at 4:00 p.m. Mom and I were so excited that we'd soon have her at home again. We could hardly wait to hear her laughter and see her smiles.

When we finally arrived to take Caylie home, she ran up and hugged me. "I get to come home today!" her excited voice sang out. "I get to take my name off the board!"

"Off what board?" I asked, wanting to share her excitement. "Your room name?"

"No, this one." She ran over to a whiteboard where her name was displayed.

One of the nurses explained that Caylie had been here the longest. Caylie would watch what happened when other patients left, and she knew what would happen when it was her turn to go. I couldn't help but smile that Caylie was curious enough to learn again.

The nurses had been wonderful friends and advocates for Caylie. They braided her hair, helped her wash her clothes, and helped her call home. I could always count on the nurses—I believe they are the glue that keeps the medical profession on track for both families and doctors.

Danielle took everything she could off my shoulders. She had contacted Dr. Fleisher's office for an appointment, a task I'd assumed would be mine to do. Danielle had also contacted Christina to set up a formal meeting of Caylie's IEP team. Beyond that, Danielle researched a behavioral therapy compatible with our insurance, and provided me with a list. Finally, she contacted the Regional Center regarding services that Caylie would need. Danielle took her job seriously, and I couldn't have been more grateful.

Caylie had a whole cartload of things to take home from

the hospital. She wiped her name off the whiteboard, and we headed for the parking area. While I loaded stuff into the car, Caylie jumped in her seat and was ready to go. As we drove over familiar roads, I watched her now and then in the rearview mirror. Her face expressed her happiness and wonder, as if she was seeing these mountains and roads for the first time.

As soon as Caylie got home, the first thing she did was pick up our little dog Gilly. Each time Caylie had been hospitalized, Gilly checked Caylie's room every day, looking to see if Caylie was back. Right away, Caylie explored her room and put her treasures from the hospital where she wanted them. I felt like a new mom again, just watching her for hours as she did everyday things.

Caylie loved putting her tree together and picking the ornaments to hang on it. To me, it was the brightest and most beautiful tree I'd ever seen. We used some of our old decorations, and I also took Caylie shopping to find new ones she wanted to add. On Christmas Day, I helped her make a video for her support team at school, who had seen Caylie through her most difficult times. She sat on her bed, her arms dancing as she sang, "We wish you a Merry Christmas," in a bright, happy voice. They responded with tearful emotes and happy faces.

A few more days, and we'd reach the end of 2018. Caylie wanted to stay up for the New Year and watch the ball fall. She remembered our getting sparkling cider in years past, and asked if we could have it again. With her sparkling cider at 9:00 p.m. in California, Caylie watched the ball fall at midnight in New York City. It was much more exciting than the Hollywood celebration would be.

"Have a good 2019, Caylie Ann," I smiled, and kissed the top of her soft blond hair.

"A good 2019, Mommy," she replied, holding her cup up as if to say 'cheers'.

MY FIGHTING INSTINCT

After Caylie's happy Christmas and New Year celebration, it was easy to believe that our nightmare might be over. At her first appointment with Dr. Fleisher, they had a pleasant conversation.

"How are you, Caylie? How was your Christmas and New Year?" he asked.

"Santa gave me art things, and I had sparkling apple juice and watched the ball drop."

"How are you sleeping?"

"Good."

"We've been trying to follow the hospital routine," I explained. "Caylie usually winds down at about 7:00 p.m. and wakes up around 5:00 a.m."

"That's about right for a teenager," Dr. Fleisher said.

"At least something's right for a change," I retorted.

"When I visited you in the hospital," Dr. Fleisher said to Caylie, "your hands were dry from washing them too many times."

"I put lotion on them," she said. "Mommy and Grandma took me to pick out my own."

After several more exchanges between Caylie and Dr.

Fleisher, he and I discussed the genetic testing results and ADHD. He had not received any information about the testing as yet. We agreed to focus on helping Caylie with her ADHD, the factor that could benefit her most in school. Dr. Fleisher wanted to see Caylie in a month.

Meanwhile, he wanted us to understand how medications can affect the patient. Dr. Fleisher also reminded me of the possible ramp-up times in which we would see progress in Caylie's treatment. My bubbles of happy feelings with a happy daughter could be fragile—the bubble could pop, and Caylie could fall back into regression at any time.

While I appreciated Dr. Fleisher's well-meant warning to shield us from the disappointment of false hopes, his words were a bombshell to me. I had days of nightmares after our visit. For many nights I lay awake, wondering if that night would be the night when Caylie would begin to regress.

Though we still didn't know what caused Caylie's regression, it was clear that she had become disabled. While I'd made some progress in learning my way around doctors and insurance politics, there was an entirely different political world in which disability services operated. I would soon discover that In-Home Support Services (IHSS) could allow me to take care of Caylie full-time while being paid as a caregiver.

Meanwhile, the Regional Center failed to process my paperwork for In-Home Services (IHSS) because my phone service was disconnected when they called. With the urgent necessity of all the contacts I had to make, I borrowed enough money to activate my phone again. As far in debt as I was, what difference would a little more make?

As Caylie's self-appointed project manager, I created new binders containing the information contacts, to have a consistent record of conversations. Also, when people wanted to argue with my facts, I was prepared, and could break down their arguments with documented information.

Of course, the moment I thought I had everything and everybody under control, I would get the bills from the hospital. Again, UCLA's charity for people like me saved us. After getting the paperwork done for the hospital payment, I sat in the Burger King parking lot and cried. I wouldn't get my graduate-school stipend for months, and by then, I'd again have no phone service, or gas for my car.

I couldn't recognize what my own life had become. How could I depend on a school stipend or a hospital charity to pay my bills? I'd always worked hard and enjoyed it. Now I worked twice as hard and had nothing to show for it. I had pawned nearly everything I had of value to care for Caylie's needs and keep the car running. As I sat there feeling sorry for myself, my recently-reconnected phone rang.

How could Ella have known to call just at that moment? As I forced myself to tell her, I didn't see how I could keep everything going, always having to fight in every direction at the same time with never any let-up. Ella didn't commiserate with me; she simply asked how much money I needed.

My conscience told me I couldn't accept her offer, couldn't take advantage of her kindness, and exploit her generosity.

"You're not asking," she said. "I'm telling you, I'm offering."

Ella sent me a three-thousand-dollar check and told me to pay everything up and take a breath.

I'll never know what I did to give myself this guardian angel, and Caylie, another grandma in her life. Ella was one of the friends who stuck by me even when I was a mess and scared of the world. No matter how bad my situation was, she kept putting me back together, piece by piece. While Ella wasn't the only one to save my car, insurance, or phone during this nightmare, she always picked up the phone when I called.

Everyone—Dr. Fleisher, our hospital and school connections, and, not least, my Dad—had emphasized that getting Caylie back in school should be Priority Number One. I wholeheartedly agreed. The first meeting regarding Caylie's new school placement, the IEP meeting, took place in late January of 2019.

Out of necessity, I took Caylie with me to the meeting. It had been just four weeks since she left the hospital, and Dr. Fleisher's reminder about the possibility of setbacks seemed to be coming true. Although Caylie seemed better in many ways, she continued talking to herself, a behavior that was supposed to be under control.

The possibility of losing my happy, sweet Caylie again when I'd just gotten her back aroused my fighting instinct. I would use every means I could to prevent regression. I wasn't about to lose without one hell of a fight. Unfortunately, there are things in the world that fighting won't fix.

There were at least nine people in the IEP meeting. As soon as we settled and started talking, Caylie wanted to leave. At first, I was ultra-apologetic, then quickly realized that no one was offended. Instead, they were treating Caylie like "a person." One of the therapists invited her to visit another office, and worked with her there.

In this meeting, I met and was impressed by James Mackey, who appeared to be a highly competent and experienced administrator in special education. As I was reviewing Caylie's experiences and her current situation for the group, Mr. Mackey commented that, in his twenty years in special education, he'd never before seen a case like Caylie's. In his experience, students who progress and do well may sometimes hit a plateau, but they don't typically regress significantly.

Mr. Mackey's comments were a welcome validation for me. I

had encountered endless skepticism and disbelief when I tried to find help and resources for Caylie. Subsequently, I often quoted him when dealing with people who didn't understand Caylie's case. At the end of the meeting, we decided we would have Caylie attending Valencia High School, and her teacher would be Lydia Bauer.

In our second appointment with Dr. Fleisher in the new year, he decided to leave Caylie's medications unchanged. We discussed the voices she continued to hear and talk to outwardly. They were her imaginary friends, she had told me. Dr. Fleisher commented that imaginary friends were possible, but they would be highly unusual at her age. Since everything about Caylie was unique, I responded that I'd go with it.

We agreed that I would observe and be prepared to report on Caylie's behavior changes, while Dr. Fleisher would pursue more information leading to the best directions to take in her treatment. He was especially pleased with and interested in her reintegration into school.

Would this fragile new beginning be here to stay? I hoped each day, but the next few weeks would tell the story.

REGIONAL CENTER AGGRAVATIONS

When Caylie started back to school, I was both terrified and excited. Would Mrs. Bauer be able to handle Caylie's unpredictable behaviors in a classroom full of other students? Or would the office call me to pick her up?

It would have been easy to talk myself into protecting Caylie from possible failure by requesting home-school options. However, I knew that a new, insightful teacher and a new classroom of peers were just what Caylie needed right now. Caylie was going back to school, and I would have a positive mindset about it.

On that first day, when Lydia Bauer came to the office to take Caylie to her classroom, she had the prettiest rustic-brown, wavy hair, and soulful brown eyes. Lydia was the friendliest, nicest, most positive person I'd met in Caylie's journey. It gave me peace of mind that Caylie was in good hands with this teacher.

I gave Lydia my contact information and all the relevant documents from the hospital. She appeared to be very confident, and not the least bit fazed by what she had heard and learned about Caylie. After a few more exchanges, Mrs. Bauer took Caylie to her classroom, and I walked back to my car alone.

For the rest of the school day, I waited, braced for that phone call, but the call never came. Each day, the reports from Gia, Lydia's aid, were consistently positive, and any time I called Lydia, she always had something positive to say about Caylie. In contrast to her experience before the last hospitalization, Caylie seemed to be thriving.

With Caylie in school part of each day, my days became more productive. I completed the In-Home Support Services application and also worked with the Regional Center to re-start Caylie's application for their services. Disability support was there, but the communication systems in each office seemed designed to make it as difficult as possible to get through to obtain it.

On February 7, we met with Dr. Fleisher again. Caylie loved school now, and she was upset at having to leave. Her appointments were upsetting me, too, because of all the school hours she was missing, hours of being a regular teen at school. Lydia would reassure me that Caylie would catch up on any missed work, and not worry: doctor appointments were standard for her students.

Dr. Fleisher could see progress in Caylie's ability to stay all day at school with other kids, but in other areas, there were concerns. Caylie was still talking to herself. It was difficult to determine whether self-talk was her method of self-regulating or responding to voices she heard. However, Dr. Fleisher noted that it could be a side-effect of one of her medications, or possibly caused by stopping a functional medicine too soon.

Frustrated that nothing we did seemed to change Caylie's overall outlook, I asked Dr. Fleisher about the genetic test results. Since genetic testing was not his area of specialization, he gave me information about making an appointment with the clinic to find out about Caylie's results.

When Caylie and I had said our goodbyes and left, I looked back at the hospital where Caylie had been just two months before. The patterns were becoming apparent—the recurring behaviors, the widening disconnects between Caylie and the world around her, and her increasing episodes of aggression. I could see it coming, and I was sure Dr. Fleisher saw it, too. Unless something changed, Caylie would be in for round three in the hospital.

While I knew it would be a victory for Caylie to be a benefit recipient at the Regional Center, their processes continued to be aggravating. Dr. Fleisher had been treating Caylie for almost two years, spanning two hospitalizations, and producing more than six hundred pages of documentation. Yet, the Regional Center still required Caylie to see, and be evaluated by, their adolescent psychiatry specialist, Dr. Betty.

For all the grief I'd given Dr. Fleisher, I still knew he was the best we could have had for Caylie's complex condition. He knew Caylie, and understood what we were going through. Dr. Betty found out quickly that Caylie didn't fit neatly into the boxes she had to check off on her forms.

I went through Caylie's history with Dr. Betty, again repeating all the information already on her computer. When my interview was over, Dr. Betty prepared to interview Caylie, saying that Caylie would be with her for about an hour. I stepped out. Seven minutes later, Caylie said she was done, and walked out.

I talked to Dr. Betty afterward while Caylie paced in the hall. Dr. Betty stated that Caylie had been uncooperative, and was possibly experiencing a psychotic episode. Obviously, the doctor had read none of the documents provided by either Dr.

Fleisher or the hospital. This visit proved the waste of time I'd expected it to be.

In my emailed report to Dr. Fleisher, I passed on Dr. Betty's view that Caylie had been in a psychotic episode. I also described how upset Caylie had been over having another psychiatrist in her life. The Regional Center's multidisciplinary team received Dr. Betty's report about a week later. She avoided discussing Caylie's findings, and my suspicions were later confirmed. Dr. Betty believed that Caylie had neither autism nor a developmental disability.

Lydia had noted that Caylie was very much out of character at school the next day, but she didn't send Caylie home. In fact, she worked out a way to help Caylie deal more constructively with her appointments. When Caylie and Lydia learned of an upcoming appointment, Caylie would write it on the class calendar. The appointment would then be an expected part of the day on which it was to occur.

There was something different about Lydia. She never gave up on Caylie in times when other teachers might have. Instead, she created ways to turn negatives into positives for Caylie and me.

As my knowledge, appreciation, and admiration for Lydia grew, we learned much in common. Her journey had started with a son who had an onset disability, and, like me, she decided to work towards her master's degree while dealing with her son's troubling situation. I decided then that Caylie and I would be Lydia's lifelong friends wherever it took us.

YOU, MRS. KAREN

n addition to everything else, the 30-day IEP meeting to set Caylie's goals for the following year was rapidly approaching. I didn't like being the center of attention, and the mere thought of this meeting was giving me anxiety. By this time, Lydia, Caylie's teacher, had become my friend and, frankly, a guide to understanding what was going on. I would call her nearly every day to go over everything in the IEP and ensure that Caylie behaved for her.

While Caylie was thriving in Lydia's class, Karen, one of the many administrators I hadn't yet met, was making things very difficult for Lydia to share her knowledge with me. Special education classrooms at Valencia High School have different levels of support, and I wanted to read about each class. At this point, I didn't know who Karen was, or her role as it pertained to Caylie, but I used Google, and found the documents she wouldn't allow Lydia to give me.

Mrs. Karen had made me more concerned about the IEP, and I called Marie from Caylie's old school, whom I trusted. Instead of being a solitary parent, I was building a team around me to challenge the status quo, because Caylie deserved the best we could offer. I knew Lydia couldn't stand up to Mrs. Karen, but I could. I was 100% done with people withholding information from me, or people like me.

I carried all six of my binders into the meeting and sat down at the table. There were about eight women around the table, and Christina from Caylie's old school was on the phone. While the first part of the meeting was primarily introductions, it was basic overviews of where Caylie had been, and where she was now.

I probably wasn't supposed to be the leader of the IEP meeting, but I had a voice, and I intended for everyone to hear it.

"Look, I'm going to start this off saying, you, Mrs. Karen, have made my life miserable trying to prepare for this meeting. Do you want to know why? My daughter two years ago regressed to behaviors that I didn't even see in her when she was a two-year-old. Do you know how scary that is? The only thing that has made me feel like I have some control over my life is stupid papers like this one! Papers that you decided were so top-secret that you wouldn't allow anyone to share them with me. Except, Google derailed your plans, and I got them anyway."

"I'm confused at…." Karen started to say.

The faces in the room looked somewhere between amused and shocked.

"I'm not done, Karen. I'm not too fond of bureaucrats; let me go around this table and point to anyone who isn't a teacher or therapist because I don't really care what you have to say. You take the credit for all the paperwork that teachers, therapists, and aids spend countless hours testing and recording. Don't think for a second that you have a pushover Mom sitting here. I will never stop fighting for Caylie, or against people like you, Karen, who come between me and information that might help me understand how best to decide for Caylie. Now, I think we can talk about an IEP."

We sat around the table for about three hours, going over the plan for Caylie and ensuring that everyone was on board with it. Lydia had included goals to build on that Caylie already knew, and we'd go from there. In the end, Caylie was going to stay with Lydia's class, as Caylie had built trust with Lydia and Gia.

As I walked away from the IEP meeting, I realized that I had reclaimed my voice for the first time in two years. I knew now that it was essential to start standing up for people on the front line working with these neurodivergent youths. To advocate for more people, I would need to study disability laws, and understand how all the organizations were interconnected.

WE'VE BEEN DOWN
THIS ROAD

At first, I had counted the hours, then the days since Caylie had walked away from school, then weeks, months, and now years. It had been two years of her life, two years when she should have been on the school dance squad, or leading a craft club, instead of struggling with a disordered mental life.

As soon as I sent out applications for the services we now could claim, I was again filling out questionnaires, providing the same information I'd made available multiple times online to related organizations and individuals. (Is anyone listening?) Mr. Kevin, my Social Security contact, wasn't amused when I read the answers to his telephoned questions from the forms I'd sent him, and which he had right in front of him.

My application to IHSS (In-Home Supportive Services) to become Caylie's paid caregiver required a live fingerprint scan, as well as certification training. The scan cost $65, and copying and mailing documents needed by Social Security cost over $75. My debt to Ella was becoming astronomical. Then the UCLA finance team sent more paperwork related to Caylie's and my living free in my parents' home in exchange for my helping the family. I'd seen my mother through breast cancer with diabetic complications, and became her driver when she gave up her license. She wrote to verify my claim and had it notarized as was required. In California, a notary costs my mom $25.

Waiting for these agency hurdles to end was a losing game. They would never end, and I had to keep moving forward in spite of them.

Meanwhile, Caylie's father and I had done our part by donating blood for the test for genetic testing. Who would tell us about the findings? Someone at UCLA must know the status of Caylie's genetic testing.

After calling the office Dr. Fleisher had suggested and not having heard back, I called three different numbers that I thought might be relevant. I started feeling as if I was going in circles. Finally, I reached back to Danielle, who had been supportive of Caylie in her most recent hospital stay. Danielle's obligations to Caylie ended when Caylie left the hospital, yet she took it upon herself to help me locate the test results. Since we would be seeing Dr. Fleisher in a few days, she said she would give him any information she discovered.

Caylie's March 4 appointment with Dr. Fleisher occurred as her behavior was again spiraling out of control. At school, she used profanity and antagonized her teacher and aid. Once, she threw her cell phone across the room when she didn't get her way. Lydia's aid simply picked up the phone and put it away for safekeeping, wisely not giving Caylie the attention she sought.

I was the only person Caylie would claw or attempt to hit at home. I studied Internet information on self-protection and defusing a hostile situation. The approach I found to work most consistently was to ask Caylie if she wanted to return to the hospital. Caylie grew to understand that her actions would have consequences.

"How are you doing today, Caylie?" Dr. Fleisher asked as Caylie, Mom, and I entered his office.

"That's BULLSHIT!" Caylie snapped.

Dr. Fleisher's quick reaction saved his shin from being squarely kicked. Caylie immediately decided she was done, and walked out the door. Mom was upset, but left to follow Caylie.

I looked over at Dr. Fleisher, shaking my head. "Is this her life forever?" I asked.

"Her brain is still growing," he said. "The reason we don't know is, we're trying to throw a dart at a moving target."

"Well, Caylie's beaten you at darts for twenty-four months running, and she's beaten the brains trust at the hospital, too," I said. "Where do we aim the next dart?"

We reviewed Caylie's medications, her overall plan, and what I should do in an emergency, and made an appointment two weeks away. Caylie appeared to be sliding toward another hospital stay, and she was now on a two-week schedule.

When Caylie went missing in February 2017, it was always in the back of my mind that she would again. I had applied for her to be a part of L.A. (Los Angeles) Found or Project Lifesaver. Project Lifesaver provides a unique radiofrequency attached to a bracelet that allows the Mental Health Team (MET) to locate a person, should they go missing. Caylie was quickly accepted into the program, as she had Autism and had run away from her school in the past.

Project Lifesaver was able to help Caylie, and I obtained this safety bracelet as there we some provided by a charity. I can't say enough about how thoughtful and kind the Project Life Saver team was then, and remains in 2022. Lydia and her team helped me make the bracelet a positive element for Caylie, as her first choice was to want it cut off her wrist.

A few years later, Caylie would have her bracelet fall off, and to my surprise, she promptly reported it to her teacher Nicole. The Project Life Saver team was terrific in getting a replacement issued. Beyond that, the L.A. County Sheriff's team was outstanding in conducting a thorough search around the school to see if the bracelet had fallen off.

It would benefit states across the country to offer this help to people with cognitive deficits. When someone you love is missing, you don't realize it's the small things that make the difference. While it is not a full-proof solution when searching for people, it gives law enforcement a better chance. People like Caylie deserve a better opportunity, given that they are dependent on caregivers for essential living.

Meanwhile, on the last day of March, I had a phone call from the office of Dr. Aaron D. Besterman at UCLA to make an appointment for Caylie. I'd heard Dr. Fleisher talk about Dr. Besterman before, but I wasn't sure why either Caylie or I required another psychiatrist. However, I made the appointment two days after our next visit to Dr. Fleisher. At that appointment, I could find out more about Dr. Besterman.

Lydia's new system of having Caylie post her appointments in view seemed to help her be ready for them at school. When she and I had made the drive to Dr. Fleisher's office, and he called us in, she went into the office without protest, and played with a deck of cards.

So far, I had nothing good to report about month twenty-five. Caylie had punched my Mom, and was being rude to Lydia at school. Also, she had developed a tremor in her hands.

Dr. Fleisher explained that tremor was a common side effect for a person on lithium.

"So, what do we do about it?" I asked. "She can't paint or write, and that's eighty percent of what makes Caylie happy."

"We can try to control it by putting her on . . ."

"We've been down this road so many times, and we're right back at square one. You haven't forgotten that Caylie is a person, right? I want her to have the . . ."

"I know Caylie is a person. Her condition is complex."

"Speaking of that, why do I have an appointment with Dr. Besterman in two days? If you have her testing results, why can't you give them to me now?"

"Genetic test results are not my specialty. Dr. Besterman does specialize in genetic analyses in psychiatry. I plan to clarify it with Dr. Besterman myself, before you and I discuss it."

More processes were becoming aggravating.

"Okay. Then what do we do about Caylie's tremors?"

After receiving Caylie's medications adjustments, I headed home with Caylie, knowing I'd be making the drive back in just two days. On the way, we stopped to pick up her bath bombs. This was our life. But the promise of actually receiving those test results gave me hope that things might change after all.

THE SLC6A17 GENE

While all I wanted to do was talk to Dr. Besterman, my project-manager side insisted on taking care of other loose ends in the week's schedule. Before leaving for the appointment, I followed up with the In-Home Support Services contact. Their contact person always answered the phone, and returned calls. They were also helpful in giving me a reasonable time frame in which to expect a decision on our application. I also checked with the Regional Center, where we had pending applications. The receptionist was apologetic that no new information was available, so I left a message for Caylie's case manager to call me.

I had often believed that we were close to discovering the cause of Caylie's regression. My cousin Melanie had shown interest in Caylie's test results, and she wanted to accompany me to the appointment. When we arrived, Dr. Besterman came out to greet us, and took us back to his office. He went right into discussing the test results, but I found his first statement mind-boggling.

"In the postnatal chromosomal microarray analysis," he said," We found everything was normal with Caylie."

"If everything was normal," I responded, "I don't think you and I would be having this conversation."

"True. In the clinical exome sequencing, we found a variant on the SLC6A17 gene, which has connections to an intellectual disability. Specifically, homozygous SLC6A17, that is, a mutation on both genes, causes autosomal regressive intellectual disability, and typically causes progressive tremor, speech impairment, and behavioral problems."

"Okay. Can you draw me a diagram?"

"Each set of parents gives their child twenty-three pairs of chromosomes. Caylie has all twenty-three pairs. On the SLC6A17 gene, there is a variant on her paternal side. We know that her father's genes were normal. After Caylie's conception, while her genes were replicating, a new variant was created."

"If I understand what you're saying, what Caylie has been through these last two years is all because of a significant gene variant."

"We know her maternal gene is functional," Dr. Besterman said. "At least, it's functional as far as the test can see. We also know it requires both genes in the SLC6A17 pair to show a variant to diagnose an intellectual disability."

"No, Dr. Besterman. You see, I believe my daughter is your evidence and your case study. My theory differs from yours. I have lived with this SLC6A17 variant for the past 732 days and counting. Prior to that, Caylie's one good gene allowed her to have a happy childhood and wonderful, happy memories. But at puberty, all the changes teens go through were too much for one gene. The brain is amazing, though. It saved those earlier memories for Caylie and for itself like a hard drive. This whole process these two years has been our trying to give the brain back what it needs and give Caylie back as much of her life as possible. Now Dr. Fleisher will know what he's looking at."

"It is a possibility. I have to stress that it is a genetic variant of unknown consequence."

"I've studied forensics both for my degrees and as a hobby. I've looked at DNA studies and evidence for years because I found it interesting. Can't you agree that the DNA evidence, plus the case study of Caylie's experience with single-gene SLC6A17, proves my theory within a margin of high probability?"

"That is a strong probability."

"That's what I thought."

After going over more information, Dr. Besterman described additional steps we could take. In truth, I couldn't afford them now, but they would be options to consider later. While here, if we took a significant walk around the UCLA campus, I could get copies of Caylie's genetic test results.

The records staff at UCLA weren't used to people asking for documents on demand, and it took a conversation with a manager to explain why I required this case file *now*. The manager understood how vital the copies were to obtaining the benefits Caylie would need for the future. Nothing had been easy, but I had never given up.

When I finally arrived home, I handed the copies to my parents and went upstairs to consider what had happened to my daughter and me in the last two years. Now I believed I had evidence that I'd been right along. Autism, ADHD, OCD, psychosis, mental illness—none of them had ever fit well, nor had any of their prescribed medications helped for long.

Officially, she had undergone a genetic mutation of unknown consequence. However, a different view is compelling for those of us who have known and experienced Caylie's history. Paired with the published study of mutations affecting both SLC6A17 genes, we believe Caylie's case represents a previously undiscovered example of a SLC6A17 genetic variant.

As soon as I was back at my desk, I collected the information Dr. Besterman had given me and began writing a template letter I would copy to IHSS, Social Security, the Regional Center, and other essential contacts. It was still early enough to get them in the mail, so I printed and signed them and took them to the nearest mailbox. IHSS seemed to be making good progress without additional evidence, but documentation of the facts might help Social Security and the Regional Center make progress.

After all these years, I had been right all along, and I was on a mission. Gone were the days when people could assume or guess at Caylie's condition, or its underlying causes. I now had proof, beyond a reasonable doubt, that any person or agency denying Caylie help would be violating her rights under the American Disabilities Act, or the Lanterman Act.

When Mom and Dad had had time to read over the information, they wanted to talk about what they had learned. Mom had been with Caylie and me to so many of our appointments. "So this means Caylie can get all those benefits you've been trying to get for her?" she asked.

"Yes. There are no more arguments they can present that stand up against genetic testing results. It's factual, and you either do or do not have a genetic variant from birth. Caylie has always had it."

Dad was listening closely. "It's finally good to know what's going on," he said. "It took a very long time."

"Yeah, it did, Dad. Too long for all of us."

After getting Caylie sorted out for the evening, I sat down at the computer to write an email to the enormous list of people who had been part of Caylie's journey, the vast team of people who had never given up on Caylie. For the first time today, I cried as I wrote it, thinking about what it had taken from so many people to get to this point.

In the week following the appointment with Dr. Besterman, everything changed for Caylie. IHHS notified me that they were sending the final paperwork to Dr. Fleisher. Soon we might get an income, and start living our lives again. I was cautiously optimistic that things were working in our favor for once.

When I contacted the Regional Center, the middle person on the phone could not help me, but I knew that it wasn't her fault. When I asked to leave a message for a director of her team, Caylie's case was quickly approved. Meanwhile, Social Security proved to be the most challenging office. But I could see the light at the end of our long tunnel, and I refused to be blocked.

With no help by phone, I gathered my information and binders and went in person to the Social Security office. There, Mr. Donald listened to my story. When he searched the files for the information, I said I'd given it to Mr. Kevin, and it was clear that Mr. Kevin had failed to enter any of it into the system. Mr. Donald took all the paperwork I'd brought and entered each relevant document into the system. Caylie's case would finally be processed.

Caylie's situation, and mine, were becoming much more accessible in some ways now that she was fully entitled to significant kinds of assistance. Still, the status of a person officially declared disabled is not simple. Circumstances involving the rights of the disabled person, the person responsible for them, and the rights of others who might encounter them in various situations, become complicated.

When I was attending the required training to become a care provider for Caylie, I'd left her at home in her grandparents' care. Unknown to them, Caylie climbed the gate in the backyard and encountered a stranger. When the woman became aware that Caylie was not talking or behaving normally, she called an agency that she thought would see that Caylie was identified, and safely returned to her home.

While the woman's actions were taken in what she believed were Caylie's best interests, to keep her safe, Caylie might have become hostile and aggressive if she was frightened. Thus, one or both of them could have been harmed. Considering the rights and best interests of everyone involved can become a complicated issue for all.

For the first time, our May visit with Dr. Fleisher was positive. Caylie was able to talk to Dr. Fleisher. While I still hoped she would someday return to the same daughter she'd once been, I was happy that she was trying. I was eager to get to know the Caylie 2.0 she had become. Dr. Fleisher said we didn't need to change her medications this month, but would re-evaluate them a month from now.

Caylie had begun to receive her SSI benefits, which allowed us to get some of the things she wanted without depending on Ella or my family. First, she wanted to shop for dresses. She loved her dresses, but had outgrown most of them. Our happy shopping trip resulted in new shorts, six new dresses, and giving the ones that no longer fit Goodwill.

We were almost there, the point at which I believed Caylie was receiving the benefits she was entitled to. It would be easy to turn loose and take our wins, but the final push might be the most helpful of all. I still hadn't received timecards to begin logging my time as an employed care provider for Caylie. After seven phone calls, I found a person who would take ownership of Caylie's case, and locate the system glitch that was blocking my application. In a few days, I would start getting my timecards.

When I received my back pay for being an IHSS caretaker, I called Ella and talked to her for a very long time. I had been preparing to figure out a repayment plan, but Ella said I did not owe her anything. Naturally, I was confused because I knew that wasn't the case. Ella explained that she believed her relationship with God had brought her to me, that she now looked at Caylie and me as bonus daughters, and she was thrilled to have been a part of our journey.

The icing on our cake was school. Caylie was thriving in Lydia's class, and she was making friends. Lydia had decided to focus on what Caylie could do successfully, and not on what frustrated her. Caylie worked on daily tasks and essential life skills, such as brushing her teeth, folding towels, and other tasks that kept her day in order. She was happy when she showed me what she had learned to do, but she would never have any idea of the joy I had when I watched her. Our lives had come full circle, and they might circle yet again. If so, this time, I was ready.

AFTERWORD

I n October 2021, I made the decision to file for conservatorship over Caylie. It was not a decision that I took lightly, or
without consulting with her doctors, family, and teachers.
While I still maintained hope that Caylie would live her life
to the fullest extent, it had become abundantly clear that she
would continue to need outside support. A limited conservatorship in California would allow me to continue legally
advocating in Caylie's best interests, as she was now over 18
years of age.

The legal paperwork and procedures required for a conser-
vativeship are relatively straightforward. There would be an
investigation into Caylie's history and needs, and a consider-
ation of what she wanted. The majority of the process went
smoothly, except for the probate investigator. I spoke with
Stan in early November, and offered several days for him to
visit our home. In Stan's own words, "I am unable to commit
to a day currently, but I will call you back."

In our first call, Stan had made a point of informing me
about a continuance, if he could not complete his report. By
December, I'd become concerned, after multiple attempts to

reach Stan resulted in his voicemail inbox no longer accepting messages. It would be easy to understand that he was busy, but our court date was quickly creeping up. Eventually, I contacted Stan's supervisor, and she stated that Stan would not be back in the office until the first business week of January.

When I finally contacted Stan in January 2022, I was far from thrilled about his lack of transparency in our previous conversations. I recapped our phone calls from 2021, and after a disrespectful interaction I ended the call. After another discussion with Stan's supervisor, we set a Zoom meeting for the following day.

On a chilly Friday in mid-January, I sat on the virtual court system waiting for Caylie's conservatorship meeting. It was the first time I'd had to reflect on the five-year journey that had brought us to this point. Each step had frequently felt like Mt. Everest, but through teamwork, tears, and tenacity, Caylie was thriving.

The entire court hearing for Caylie's limited conservatorship took less than ten minutes. With approvals from the regional center, investigators, and overwhelmingly supportive evidence, I became Caylie's conservator. My eyes teared up when the judge made the order. In reality, a conservatorship was for everyone else; for me, it meant I could keep being a voice for Caylie that people would have to listen to: her Mom.

When I decided to write our journey, it was for the simple reason that I knew there had to be other parents like me who felt alone. I felt compelled to help others know that the nightmare they are living through does have an end—or at least a point of eventually knowing where things stand. No matter how fragile, that hope is a lifeline to cling to when nothing makes sense.

Another reason highlighted the lack of respect for teachers in bureaucratic policies, combined with no salary increase for several consecutive years. In truth, I never gave school board meetings any attention before my daughter became disabled. When I read that the teachers who gave Caylie their all would again receive no cost-of-living increase, I was furious.

We are blessed to live in a community well-funded through our high taxes, but to my knowledge, those taxes have not translated into increasing teachers' wages. Instead, the superintendents in recent years have used forecasting that has not come to pass in actuality.

In early 2021, lawmakers in the United States voiced their concerns about conservatorship over the last several years, because of one famous person. One person should never be the only reason a law such as conservatorship is changed. In writing this book, I hope it does get into the hands of lawmakers to give them an authentic, brutal look at what someone who will need conservatorship has gone through. It's the side that is often not brought to media attention, because it's not perfect, nor does it paint a glamorous image.

In closing, there is no guide on being a parent that prepares you for the journey Caylie and I have experienced. I have come to terms with the fact that Caylie may never return to the young woman she once was, but today she's happy, healthy, and living her best life. As a parent, I couldn't ask for anything more. Five years ago, my journey started as I was looking for Caylie, and as life would have it, I found Caylie: and together, we found so much more.